Contents

Introduction

The Impact of COVID 19 on Regsitering powers of Attorney.

POW   Y

PETER WADE

Emerald Guides
www.straightforwardco.co.uk

Emerald Guides

****

Introduction

To grant someone power of attorney is a fundamental requirement, mainly affecting people who are finding it increasingly difficult to manage their affairs, usually elderly people who need to instruct someone they trust to manage their affairs.

However, it is by no means restricted to elderly. It could be, for example, someone who for some other reason has lost the ability to manage their affairs, such as someone who is ill or has been in an accident.

This revised edition of Powers of Attorney is up to date to 2020 and should prove an invaluable guide to the various areas related to power of attorney, whether it be Ordinary Power of Attorney, Lasting Power or Enduring Power of Attorney. Much of the emphasis in this book is on lasting Power of Attorney.

There is a new section in the book dealing with Powers of Attorney in Scotland and also Northern Ireland as these countries have their own different versions of the law and powers of attorney. Overall though, the practice amounts to the same thing-that is entrusting someone else with the management of affairs and the management of assets.

Of course, at the time of writing it is important to make reference to the situation with making and registering Powers of attorney during COVID 19. The issue is one of the mechanics of how to carry out all of the due processes during a period of restrictions, which currently seem to have no end in sight. The advice below should be borne in mind when reading through the book, particularly the sections on registering a Power of Attorney.

Making and registering an LPA during the coronavirus outbreak

If you want to make an LPA now, you can as long as you follow government guidance on social distancing and self-isolating, and observe national restrictions. As we will emphasise throughout the book, making a lasting power of attorney (LPA) is an important decision that you should think about carefully. An LPA needs to be signed and witnessed by several people.

As you will see, once the LPA has been signed, you need to send it for registration. It may then be around 8 weeks before you get the registered LPA back and can start using it. This includes a 4 week waiting period required by law. Currently, the Office of the Public Guardian is experiencing delays registering and returning LPAs.

You can still make an LPA during this time. There are other ways people can make decisions for you that are quicker to get in place. These may be useful while you're waiting for an LPA to be registered or if you're self-isolating and need someone to carry out bank transactions for you.

How do I make an LPA during the COVID-19 outbreak?

If you want to make an LPA now, you can still do so as long as you follow government guidance on social distancing. self-isolating and observe national restrictions if they are still in force.

This guidance is for people making an LPA in England and Wales only. There is separate guidance for people making an LPA in Scotland and Northern Ireland. for Scotland go to: https://www.publicguardian-scotland.gov.uk. For Northern Ireland go to: https://www.nidirect.gov.uk/articles/managing-your-affairs.

Signing and witnessing the LPA

You should follow government guidance on social distancing and national restrictions to ensure that you satisfy requirements when signing and witnessing an LPA.

Do not:

- use digital signatures - the document must be printed out and signed by hand with a black pen
- send people photocopies or scans of the LPA to sign - everyone must sign the same, original document

- ask people to send you a scan or photocopy of the page they've signed The Office of the Public Guardian cannot register an LPA that includes scans or copied pages

Witnessing the donor and attorneys' signatures

Witnessing must be done in person. You will need to follow government guidance on social distancing and national restrictions at all times when signing the forms.

Rules on witnessing

The witness must:

- be shown the blank signature and date box before they're signed
- have a clear view of the person signing the LPA, so they can see the signature being made
- be shown the completed signature and date box immediately afterwards

Signatures must be witnessed in person.

If the donor cannot sign the LPA

If the donor is not able to use a pen and cannot sign the LPA, someone else can sign on their behalf. The donor and 2 other people must be there in person to witness the signature being made. The 2 witnesses must also sign the LPA. You must follow all the rules on witnessing in accordance with the government social distancing guidance and national restrictions

Make sure the LPA is signed in the right order

It's very important that the LPA is signed in the right order. If it's not, it cannot be registered it. The donor may have to make a new LPA, get it signed again, and pay another application fee.

The certificate provider and donor conversation

The certificate provider must talk to the donor about the LPA to make sure the donor understands it and is not being pressured to make it. It is recommend this conversation happens face to face, but you must consider the government social distancing guidance and national restrictions. If this must be over phone or a video call, the certificate provider should make sure the call is private.

Think carefully about who should be sent the registered LPA

When you make an LPA, you'll be asked to say who will be the 'correspondent'. This is the person the Office of the Public Guardian will send the registered LPA to.

If you think you might need to use the LPA very soon after it's registered, think carefully about who should be the correspondent to make sure the person who needs it has access to it. Organisations, such as banks and care homes, will want to see this original registered LPA when an attorney wants to make decisions on the donor's behalf.

If you do not have access to a printer

You can ask a friend or family member to print the forms and post them to you. You can also ask the Office of the Public Guardian to post you the LPA application forms. Their telephone number is: 0300 456 0300

How you can help the Office of the Public Guardian to register your LPA as quickly as possible:

- Use the online service to make the LPA and pay the application fee by card rather than cheque. Although you'll still need to print the completed forms to sign and then post them, it will take us less time to register your LPA. This is because cheques take much longer to process than card payments. If you make the LPA online, you'll also be able to track the progress of your application through the service without needing to contact the Office.
- If the donor and attorney have email addresses, include them on the LPA form. This will make it much quicker for us to contact them if there are any issues.

Double check your forms before sending them in. Avoid common mistakes, by making sure:

- the LPA is signed in the right order
- you send the Office all pages of the LPA, even those you have not needed to complete
- you post the original document – the Office cannot accept scans or photocopies
- you carefully read the guidance on making LPAs

It is hoped that this book will prove useful to those who read it and who are seeking further guidance.

****

Ch. 1

Ordinary/Lasting Powers of Attorney

Ordinary powers of attorney

An ordinary power of attorney allows one or more person, known as your attorney, to make financial decisions on your behalf. It's only valid while you still have the mental capacity to make your own decisions. You may want to set one up if, for example:

- you need someone to act for you for a temporary period, such an when you're on holiday or in hospital
- you're finding it harder to get out and about to the bank or post office, or you want someone to be able to access your account for you
- you want someone to act for you while you're able to supervise their actions.

You can limit the power you give your attorney so that they can only deal with certain assets, for example, your bank account but not your home. An ordinary power of attorney is only valid while you have the mental capacity to make your own decisions. If you want someone to be able to act on your behalf if there comes a time when you don't have the mental capacity to make your own decisions you should consider setting up a lasting power of attorney.

Lasting power of attorney

Lasting Power of Attorney is a legal document which gives authority to another person to make decisions on your behalf. This is obviously someone you can trust to make decisions on your behalf. The Attorney you choose will be able to make decisions for you when you become lacking in mental capacity or simply no longer wish to do so. There are two types of Lasting Power of Attorney. There is:

- Property and Financial Lasting Power of Attorney, which allows your attorney to deal with your property and finances.
- Health and Welfare which allows your attorney to make care decisions on your behalf when you lack mental capacity to do so.

A Lasting Power of Attorney cannot be used until it is registered with the Office of the Public Guardian. By having a Lasting Power of Attorney you are ensuring a safe way of having decisions made for you. The following reasons for this are:

- It has to be registered with the Office of the Public Guardian before it can be used

- You can choose someone to provide a 'certificate', which means they confirm that you understand the significance and purpose of what you're agreeing to. This is normally a solicitor or legal expert

- You can choose who gets told about your Lasting Power of Attorney when it is registered (so they have an opportunity to raise concerns). This may be a relative or someone close to you

- Your signature and the signatures of your chosen attorneys must be witnessed

- Your attorney(s) must follow the Code of Practice of the Mental Capacity Act 2005 and act in your best interests

The Office of the Public Guardian provides helpful support and advice

****

Ch. 2

The Mental Capacity Act 2005

The Attorney's must follow the code of the Mental Capacity Act 2005. Copies of this can be obtained from direct.gov.uk/mental capacity.

The main principles of the Act are:

- They must assume that you can make your own decisions

- They must help you to make as many decisions as you can

- Your Attorney's must make decisions and act in your best interests when you are unable to make the decisions yourself.

What is Mental Capacity?

In everyday life we make decisions about various matters in our lives. We call this ability to make these decision 'Mental Capacity'. Some people may experience some difficulty in making decisions and this may be due to various reasons such as, a mental health problem, a learning disability or have had a stroke or brain injury.

The Mental Capacity Act of 2005 has more guidance on how to assess someone's ability to make decisions

This act covers decisions in areas such as property and financial affairs and health and welfare etc. It also covers everyday decisions such as personal care.

The Act also sets out five principles that are the basis of the legal requirement of the Act.

Unless it can be proved otherwise, every adult has the right to make their own decisions. All available help must be given before they are deemed not to be able to make their own decisions.

Any decision made for a person who is unable to so for themselves must be done in their best interests. Any decisions made for someone else should not restrict their basic rights and freedoms.

The Court of Protection has the power to make decisions about whether someone lacks mental capacity. It can also appoint deputies to act and make decisions on behalf of someone who is unable to do so on their own.

****

Ch. 3

Enduring Powers of Attorney (EPA's)

No more Enduring Powers of Attorney may be created after the 1st October 2007, but there are Enduring Powers of Attorney which are in existence and they are perfectly legally valid.

It is a legal document by which the Donor give the legal right to one or more Attorney's to manage the Donor's property and financial affairs. The document allows the Attorney's to do anything that the Donor would have been able to do for themselves.

General Powers of Attorney

A General Power of Attorney can still be created but this ends when the Donor lacks mental capacity, but an Enduring Power of Attorney continues even once this capacity no longer exists. Under an enduring Power of Attorney, once the Donor becomes mentally incapable the Attorney will need to apply to Register the Enduring Power of Attorney with the OPG. Enduring Powers of Attorney were created under the Enduring Powers of Attorney Act 1985 which has been repealed by the Mental Capacity Act of 2005. The capacity to create an EPA was assumed to exist unless it was proven to the contrary.

If a person has mental capacity then Enduring Power of Attorney can be used like an Ordinary Power of Attorney. Once the mental capacity has lost this has to be registered.

Under an Enduring Power of Attorney, Attorney's may be appointed jointly or jointly and severally. Whereas with a single Attorney, that Attorney should sign on each occasion where two or more Attorneys are appointed they can be joint or joint and several. Jointly means both Attorney's need to sign on every occasion. Joint and Several means that either of the Attorneys could both sign but are not required to sign on each occasion. Both are not required to sign on each occasion.

****

Ch. 4

The Difference Between Enduring Powers Of Attorney and Lasting Powers of Attorney

---

As has been stated, there cannot now be created an Enduring Power of Attorney, since the 1st of October 2007. However, they are still in existence.

With a Lasting Power of Attorney, it must contain names or persons who the donor wishes to be notified of any application and also must contain the Certificate that the donor understands the purpose of the instrument.

Decisions made under an LPA/EPA

Under an EPA the attorneys can do anything with the Donor's property and financial affairs, but cannot make decisions about the Donor's personal welfare.

Under an LPA the Attorney's can make decisions about property and financial affairs and personal welfare, including refusing consent to treatment. The latter applies only if the Donor lacks, or that the Attorney reasonably believes that the Donor lacks mental capacity.

****

Ch. 5

Who Can Create a Lasting Power of Attorney?

_____

Anyone can create a Lasting Power of Attorney and it can also be described as the Capacity, that is those who are able make a Lasting Power of Attorney.

The Donor (the person making the LPA) has to be at least 18 years of age and has to have the mental capacity to execute under the Mental Health Act 2005.

The definition of lack of capacity is if a person lacks capacity in relation to a matter if at the material time he is unable to make a decision for himself in relation to the matter because of an impairment or of a disturbance in the functioning of the mind or brain. This may be either a temporary or permanent disturbance.

There is a presumption that a person can be assumed to have mental capacity unless it is established that he lacks capacity.

All persons over the age of 18 years of age are presumed to be capable of making their own decisions. The standard of proof is on a balance of probabilities. The Lasting Power of Attorney includes a certificate by a person of a prescribed description that at the time the Donor executes the instrument that;

The Donor understood the purpose of the instrument and the scope of the authority conferred under it.

No fraud or undue pressure is used to induce the Donor to create an LPA

There is nothing else which would prevent an LPA from being created from the instrument.

The current Fees, currently in 2020 for Registering a Lasting Power of Attorney are £82 and the fees for resubmitting an LPA for registration £41 .

The Lasting Power of Attorney can be cancelled at any time as long as the person giving it has mental capacity to cancel.

What happens if there is no LPA?
If there is no LPA then an application will need to be made to the Court of Protection at considerably more cost and with no guarantee that the right person will be appointed as the Deputy as it is named.

Ch. 6

Creating a Lasting Power of Attorney

_____

The forms can be found on the Ministry of Justice website.These forms are also contained in the appendix to this book. Please bear in mind the advice about registering during COVID 19, set out in the introduction. The problems caused by the pandemic affect all legal services.

The Registration must be done correctly and if there is a defect in the form may result in the refusal of the registration.

Once the LPA has been signed errors cannot be simply corrected although the OPG may allow certain amendments.

Executing the LPA – it must be signed by the Donor, the Certificate provider and the Attorneys in the correct order.

Execution by the Donor or the Attorneys must take place in the presence of a witness.

Restrictions on who can act as a witness are:

- The Donor and the Attorney must not witness each other's signature.

It is also suggested that neither the Donor's spouse or civil partner witness the LPA.

****

Ch. 7

When Can it be Used – Or When Does the Instrument Come into Effect?

_____

An LPA only comes into effect when the Donor has become mentally incapable and will remain in operation provided it is registered.

Under an LPA it only becomes operable once it is registered with the Office of the Public Guardian.

This can take a number of weeks for registration to complete and the LPA cannot be used until this has been completed

The Office of the Public Guardian will give notice of the registration application to you or the Attorney(s). They will allow a period of five weeks waiting period in which you or the Attorney's may object to the registration. If the Donor objects to the registration then it can only go ahead if the Court is satisfied that the donor lacks the capacity to object.

****

Ch. 8

Who Can be an Attorney?

_____

Anyone over the age of 18 having mental capacity can be an Attorney, but there are factual grounds which may stop this such as:

- The Attorney is bankrupt.

- That the Attorney lacks capacity

- The Attorney has signed a Disclaimer

It is important to realise that anyone you appoint as your Attorney under a Lasting Power of Attorney will need, at some point to make important decisions for you.

You may decide to appoint a solicitor or other legal expert as an Attorney, however you must bear in mind that professional people may charge for their services. If however you choose a friend or relative as an Attorney they may be able to claim out of pocket expenses. However they cannot charge for their time unless the Donor has already agreed this on the LPA form. A donor can choose to have more than one Attorney which means that they can act together or independently and you will need to decide this. The obvious advantage of this is that it is harder for one Attorney to commit fraud and or act against the interests of the Donor.

If something happens to one of the Attorneys, and they are unable to act, there will be another one or two who can act as well. You may however have a good reason not to do this.

You can choose up to five people who can be named but one is sufficient. These can include family members but not your lawyers or certificate providers.

****

Ch. 9

Duties of an Attorney Under a Lasting Power of Attorney

The Attorney's need to apply to the Court of Protection for Registration if they have reason to believe that the Donor has become mentally incapable.

Under a Lasting Power of Attorney they must act in accordance with the Mental Capacity Act 2005 and in the Donor's best interest and with regard to the Code of Practice.

The Attorney has the duty to act in the scope of the Lasting Power of Attorney subject to the MCA 2005 particularly the principles and best interests.

In addition they have a duty of care. This is one of care to:

- Carry out the Donor's instructions
- Not to take advantage of the position of the Attorney
- Not to delegate unless authorised to do so

- Of good faith
- Confidentiality to comply with directions of the Court of Protection
- Not to disclaim without notifying the Donor or the other Attorneys and the Public Guardian and complying with relevant guidance.

In relation to property and financial affairs there is an additional duty to keep account and keep the Donor's money and property separate from their own.

If the Attorneys are professional Attorneys they should demonstrate a higher degree of care and skill and they must also follow their professional rules and standards.

****

Ch. 10

Gifts

In connection with a Property and Financial Affairs Lasting Power of Attorney, the Attorney's have limited authority to make gifts of a donor's money or property if the recipient of the gift is related to or connected with the Donor or a charity to which the Donor actually made gifts or might be expected to make gifts if they had capacity.

A gift to a charity may be made at any time of the year, but a Gift to an individual might be of a seasonal nature, i.e. birth, marriage anniversary.

The value of the gift must not be unreasonable having regard to the circumstances. Gifts are not permitted to be made by the Attorney of your assets unless:

a) The recipient of the gift is an individual who is related to or connected with you or a charity to which you actually made gifts or might be expected to make gifts.

b) The timing of the gift must be of a seasonable nature or made on the occasion of a birth or marriage/civil partnership or on the anniversary of a birth or marriage/civil partnership.

c) The value of the gift must not be unreasonable having regard to all the circumstances and in particular the size of your estate.

If you wish you can totally restrict or exclude the ability to make any gifts or limit these.

The Court of Protection can authorise the Attorney to act so as to benefit themselves or otherwise provided there are no restrictions in the LPA itself and the Court is satisfied that this would be in your best interests.

****

Ch. 11

When Should the LPA Be Registered?

_____

Lasting Power of Attorney Registration
When should my LPA be registered?
Your LPA can be registered at any time after it has been completed and properly signed. The advantage to having it registered right away is that the LPA can be used by the Attorney whenever it is needed. If a long time passes before your LPA is registered, your circumstances may have changed and your LPA may no longer reflect your needs. If this is the case, you will not be able to modify your signed and completed LPA. You will have to create a new LPA.

Who can register my LPA?
Either the donor or the attorney may apply to register the LPA as long as the proper forms have been completed and all people who are to be notified have been notified.

Who must be notified of the application to register the LPA?
All named persons identified on the LPA must be notified. If you are

an attorney making the application, you are not required to notify the Donor (although its strongly recommended that you discuss your intention to register with the donor). The Office of the Public Guardian will formally notify the Donor.

If I am an attorney acting together with another attorney, can I make an application on my own?

No, all attorneys appointed together must make an application together.

If I am an attorney acting together and independently with another attorney, can I make an application on my own?

You may make an application on your own, however it is a good idea to discuss your intention to apply for registration with all other attorneys. If the other attorneys know and approve of the registration, then your registration is less likely to encounter any challenges.

What forms should I use to register an LPA?

You require the form LP1F (see appendix for sample 3 main forms) for registering a Financial LPA: Form LP1H for registering a Health and welfare LPA: Form LP3 for Notifying people of a LPA and form LPA120 which indicates fees and also reduced fees for those on low income. Form LP12 is very useful as it is a complete guide to registering a LPA. You should go to www.gov.uk/power-of-attorney.

If I have an LPA for Personal Welfare and an LPA for Property and Financial Affairs will I require two different applications?

Yes, you will need a separate set of registration forms for each Power of Attorney as indicated above.

Who can object to my LPA being registered?

You, your Attorney and the individuals you have selected to be notified are allowed to object to your LPA being registered.

What are the prescribed grounds for objecting to the registration of a LPA?

The prescribed grounds for objecting to the registration of a LPA are as follows:

- the Powers created by the LPA are not valid (e.g. the person objecting does not believe the Donor had capacity to make an LPA);

- the power created by LPA no longer exists (e.g. the Donor revoked it at a time when he/she had capacity to do so);

- Fraud or undue pressure was used to induce the Donor to make the LPA; or the Attorney proposes to behave in a way that would contravene his/her authority or would not be in the Donor's best interests.

- Any objection that is raised will need to be supported with factual evidence.

How much does it cost to register an LPA? The fee for registering an LPA is currently set at £82 (2020) with a repeat application £41. The fee is payable by the person seeking to register the LPA and is recoverable from the Donor's funds. Certain individual may be entitled to exemptions or remissions of fees. For more information on fees, exemptions from fees and fee remissions go to the Office of the Public Guardian.

****

Ch. 12

Abuse of Powers of Attorney

The function of the Court of Protection is to make sure that the person who is lacking in mental capacity has their best interests determined at all times and that there are no abuse of powers. It has the following powers:

- To make declarations as to whether a Person (P) has capacity to make a particular decision ((Mental Capacity Act 2005, section 15(1)).
- To make declarations as to the lawfulness or otherwise of an act done, or yet to be done, in relation to P (section 15 (1)(c)).
- To make single one-off orders (section 16(2)(a)), such as an order authorising the execution of a statutory will on behalf of an elderly person with Vascular dementia or Alzheimer's disease.
- To appoint a deputy to make decisions in relation to the matters in which P lacks the capacity him or herself, whether they relate to P's property and affairs or personal welfare (section 16 (2)(b)).

- To resolve various issues involving Lasting Powers of Attorney (sections 22 and 23) and Enduring Powers of Attorney (schedule 4).
- To make a declaration as to whether an advance decision to refuse treatment exists, is valid, or is applicable to a particular treatment (section 26(4)).
- To exercise an appellate jurisdiction in Deprivation of Liberty Safeguards (DOLS) cases.

What powers does it have?

The Court of Protection has the powers to:

- Decide whether a person has capacity to make a particular decision for themselves;
- Make declarations, decisions or orders on financial or welfare matters;
- Appoint deputies;
- Decide whether a Lasting Power of Attorney or Enduring Power of Attorney is valid;
- Remove deputies or attorneys who fail to carry out their duty;
- Hear cases concerning objections to register an LPA or EPA.

But once the Court of Protection has appointed a suitable other person called a "Deputy" to act on their behalf, that Deputy will be able to take control of their bank accounts.

They will be unfrozen and they will also be able to take control of any properties or interests to enable their sale or other transaction in the best interest of the incapable person.

If a person does not have sufficient mental capacity to make a LPA, then a member of the family can make an application to the Court of Protection for authority to act on that person's behalf with regard to their financial affairs. Where there is no family, a professional adviser such as a solicitor or the Local Authority may make this application instead. If successful, the applicant will be appointed as that person's Deputy.

****

Ch. 13

Revoking the Power of Attorney

The Court of Protection may confirm or revoke the registered Enduring Power of Attorney if the Donor is mentally capable of making such a revocation.

Similarly with the Lasting Power of Attorney, the dissolution or Annulment of a marriage or civil partnership will terminate the appointment of an Attorney or revoke the Power.

What is a "Revocation of Power of Attorney"? Questions and answers.

A: A Revocation of Power of Attorney is a legal document signed by or on behalf of a person who granted a Power of Attorney (the Donor). It states that the donor is cancelling the powers that were given to another person (the Attorney) in an earlier Power of Attorney. The document provides written confirmation that the donor has revoked the Power of Attorney that was previously granted.

Q: Why would I want to revoke a Power of Attorney I previously granted?

A: Some reasons why you may wish to revoke a Power of Attorney include:

- The Power of Attorney is no longer necessary as you are now able to act on your own behalf;
- You no longer trust the person who is acting on your behalf (your Attorney);
- You have found a more suitable candidate to act as your Attorney;
- It is no longer practical to have your Attorney acting on your behalf (e.g. your Attorney no longer resides in the same jurisdiction as you do); and
- The purpose of the Power of Attorney has been fulfilled and you no longer need an Attorney to act for you.

Q: Is it necessary for me to have a written Revocation of Power of Attorney?

A: A Power of Attorney is a powerful legal document which can enable an Attorney to do almost anything with your property (depending on the powers you have granted in the Power of Attorney document). A revocation of a Power of Attorney is not effective against the Attorney or any third party (e.g. bank) until notice of the revocation has been received by that party. Consequently, it is a good idea to have a written document as evidence of your revocation to make sure there is no doubt as to your intention to revoke the power.

Q: When can I revoke my Power of Attorney?

A: A Power of Attorney can be revoked at any time, regardless of the termination date specified in the document, as long as the Donor is mentally capable. (Note: there are some exceptions, but these apply only to "binding" Powers of Attorney.

Q: Can I still revoke my Power of Attorney if I become incompetent?

A: An ordinary power of attorney is automatically revoked if the person who made it is found to be incompetent, but a durable/enduring power of attorney can only be revoked by the person who made it while that person is mentally competent.

Q: Do I have to specify why I am revoking my Power of Attorney?

A: You are not required to explain why you are revoking your Power of Attorney. As long as you are mentally capable, you can revoke your Power of Attorney for any reason (or for no reason).

Q. How will my Revocation of Power of Attorney become effective?

A: In order to give effect to your Revocation you must complete the following steps:

- Have your Revocation witnessed or acknowledged before a notary;

- Provide a copy of your Revocation to your Attorney and ask him/her to return all of his/her copies of the Power of Attorney;
- Provide a copy of your Revocation to any financial institutions or any other third parties where your Power of Attorney may have been used; and
- Provide a copy of your Revocation to any agency where your Power of Attorney has been recorded (e.g. County Clerk's Office, deed registry or land titles office).

****

Ch. 14

Functions of The Office of The Public Guardian

The Office of the Public Guardian protects people who are lacking in mental capacity. All Lasting Powers of Attorney and Enduring Powers of Attorney are registered at the OPG.

The role of the Public Guardian is to protect people who lack mental capacity to look after themselves and they do this by various means:

- By registering Lasting and Enduring Powers of Attorney

- By working with organisations such as social services, if the person is receiving social care and supervising deputies

- Making sure that the attorneys and the deputies are acting correctly and also investigating any concerns that arise

- Decide whether a power of attorney is valid and remove deputies or attorneys who fail to carry out their duties.

The current details for access to the Office of the Public Guardian are as follows:

Emailcustomerservices@publicguardian.gsi.gov.uk

Telephone 0300 456 0300

****

Ch. 15

Functions of The Court of Protection

Please bear in mind that the operations of the Court of Protection have also been affected by COVID 19. The Court will determine whether an application is urgent or not and this will depend on the evidence presented to Court. The Court says that health and welfare cases *will* be done. However, "Court of Protection – property and affairs" cases fall into the final category that the Court 'will do their best to do.' These are the most common cases in the Court of Protection and include deputyship applications.

The Court deals with a huge number of routine deputyship applications in a typical year but due to coronavirus restrictions and pressures on staffing, it is now expected that there will be further delays. For more guidance go to: https://www.judiciary.uk/.../court-of-protection-guidance-covid-

What is the function of the Court of Protection?
Most of us take for granted that we have the ability to manage our own affairs, however should something happen, for example a stroke causing paralysis or an illness such as dementia, and that

ability was diminished, the Court of Protection has the jurisdiction to make decisions on an affected person's behalf or appoint a suitable person to do so. The Court of Protection has the powers to:

- Decide whether a person has capacity to make a particular decision for themselves;
- Make declarations, decisions or orders on financial or welfare matters;
- Appoint deputies;
- Decide whether a Lasting Power of Attorney or Enduring Power of Attorney is valid;
- Remove deputies or attorneys who fail to carry out their duty;
- Hear cases concerning objections to register an LPA or EPA.

What does the Court of Protection actually do?

Once a person is classed as incapable and unable to manage their financial affairs, any bank that holds monies for them may freeze their accounts. This is perfectly legal and correct and is done to prevent any third party from fraudulently operating the accounts. Or, if a person should need to move house or into residential care but is classed as mentally incapable, they are legally prevented from signing the legal paperwork in order to sell their property. But once the Court of Protection has appointed a suitable other person called a "Deputy" to act on their behalf, that Deputy will be able to take control of their bank accounts and they will be unfrozen and they will also be able to take control of any properties or interests to enable their sale or other transaction in the best interest of the incapable person.

If that person had at some time in the past made an Enduring Power of Attorney (EPA) or Lasting Power of Attorney (LPA), then the Attorney named in that document can begin to act on the person's behalf. If that person has no EPA or LPA in place, they should take legal advice as to whether they are well enough to make a LPA. There is a strict legal test for ascertaining if a person has sufficient mental capacity to make a power of attorney. If your solicitor is unsure, they may ask for a doctor to make an assessment.

If a person does not have sufficient mental capacity to make a LPA, then a member of the family can make an application to the Court of Protection for authority to act on that person's behalf with regard to their financial affairs. Where there is no family, a professional adviser such as a solicitor or the Local Authority may make this application instead. If successful, the applicant will be appointed as that person's Deputy.

Once a Deputy is appointed, they will be able to take control of the incapable person's finances and property. The Deputy must always act in the incapable person's best interests and comply with the

Mental Capacity Act 2005 and related Code of Practice. The Deputy must keep accurate records of his dealings with their assets and income and submit an annual account to the OPG. There are three levels of supervision and the Court will set this. It is also necessary for the Deputy to take out an insurance policy to cover any negligent acts.

There are prescribed application forms which must be completed to begin a Deputyship application. Notice must be given to the person's close relatives and any person with an interest in their welfare such as their unmarried partner or carer. These persons have a right to raise any concerns about the proposed Deputy's suitability to act. The Court can refuse an application by someone they consider too elderly to act or someone who has a poor history of managing their own finances. The process takes approximately six months depending on how busy the Court is. It is therefore important to consult a solicitor at an early stage if you suspect that a relative is becoming unable to manage their affairs.

It is possible for a Deputy to be appointed to make personal welfare decisions on an incapable person's behalf, e.g. where they should live or what medical treatment they should receive. However, the Court will only appoint a Deputy in extremely limited circumstances such as where there is disagreement amongst family members/carers or where their medical condition means that treatment decisions must be made frequently. Laws exist (see Section 5 of the Mental Capacity Act 2005 and the Code of Practice) to authorise the person responsible for the incapable person's care to make day-to-day personal welfare decisions on their behalf.

Aside from Deputyship decisions, applications can also be made by Attorneys or Deputies to the Court of Protection for permission to make gifts of the incapable person's assets in order to save inheritance tax or for permission to make a Will on their behalf if they should lack the ability to do so.

Joint or joint and several attorneys
With an Enduring Power of Attorney they may act jointly or jointly and severally, similarly with a Lasting Power of Attorney. If the donor fails to specify the appointment it is assumed to be jointly.

****

Ch. 16

The Donor's Ability to Make Decisions

Under an Enduring Power of Attorney both the Donor and the Attorney have authority to make decisions once it has been registered.

Under a Lasting Power of Attorney the Donor can still carry on making decisions provided that they have the capacity.

With regards to personal welfare, the Attorney can make personal welfare decisions once the donor is incapable of making such decisions.

****

Ch. 17

Registering

With a Lasting Power of Attorney the person named by the Donor or as being entitled to receive notification needs to be notified.

The Lasting Power of Attorney is not created until it has been registered with the Office of the Public Guardian. It cannot be used until it has been registered. The Lasting Power of Attorney can be registered at any time after the forms have been completed and signed by all those who need to sign.

The implication of not registering the Lasting Power of Attorney should be carefully considered. For example in health and welfare Lasting Power of Attorney if there was a medical emergency the attorney's would not be authorised to act until it was registered. A fee will be payable for the registration of the Lasting Power of Attorney and a separate fee for both the property and affairs under the personal welfare even if they are made by the same party. Once registered the property and financial affairs Lasting Power of Attorney can be used while the donor still has capacity unless it is specified otherwise.

The health and welfare Lasting Power of Attorney can only be used when the donor no longer has capacity.

There is no time limit for making the application to register the Lasting Power of Attorney and it can be made by the Donor or the Attorneys. Various parties need to be notified for an application to register the Lasting Power of Attorney. If the donor decides not to include anyone to be notified then a second person will need to provide an additional certificate.

By naming a person to be notified this is a safeguard. The donor or the Attorneys making the application to register must give notice in the prescribed form to everyone named by the Donor.

The Registered Lasting Power of Attorney will be stamped on every page by the OPG. The OPG are responsible of maintaining a register of all Lasting Powers of Attorney, Enduring Powers of Attorney and Court Appointed Deputies.

A Registered Lasting Power of Attorney is a public document and will be available to anyone who applies to search the register.

****

Ch. 18

Disclosure of the Donor's Will

_____

There is a general duty to keep the client's affairs confidential, however the Attorney may need to know the contents of the donor's will so as not to act contrary to the intentions of the donor, i.e. sale of an asset specifically left to someone.

The disclosure of the Donor's Will should be discussed at the time of making the Lasting Power of Attorney and instructions should be obtained.

If there is no authority the Attorney's should apply to the Court of Protections for a specific order for the contents of the Will to be disclosed

The Attorney's have a duty to keep the donor's affairs confidential including the contents of the Will.

****

Ch. 19

Powers of Attorney-Scotland

A Power of Attorney in Scotland

Power of Attorney (POA) allows a person to choose someone else to deal with third parties, such as banks or the local council, on their behalf, should they be unable to do so in the future.

In Scotland, there are three types of Power of Attorney:

- Continuing Power of Attorney (CPA)
- Welfare Power of Attorney (WPA)
- Combined Power of Attorney, which is a combination of a CPA and WPA.

Continuing Power of Attorney (CPA)

This form of Power of Attorney allows someone (the 'granter') to appoint someone else to look after their property and financial affairs immediately, continuing into incapacity or if they become mentally incapable. It can also contain welfare powers, for example, to determine where a person should live should they need to move due to changing levels of care need. Welfare powers can only come into effect on incapacity.

A CPA must be registered with the Scottish Office of the Public Guardian to be effective.

Welfare Power of Attorney (WPA)

This Power of Attorney enables an attorney(s) to make decisions about a persons health and welfare after they become incapable. These powers can include deciding where they will live and personal issues, such as medical treatment and personal care. Their attorney(s) can't intervene while they have capacity to make the decision for themselves.

Setting up a Power of Attorney in Scotland

Setting up a CPA or a WPA is straightforward. A person can do it themselves or through a solicitor or will writer. If a person chooses to use a solicitor or will writer, they always ask for written confirmation of their fees beforehand.

When setting things up, a person can stipulate which 'powers' they want to give; for example, they might only want their attorney to deal with their bills, but not to have the power to sell their property, or they may only want the attorney to deal with their affairs once they start to lose capacity. A person can give 'power' to one or more people and they are known as the 'granter'. It's important that they choose people they can trust to act in their best interests. If they are appointing more than one person, they must decide if they will make decisions:

separately or together: sometimes called 'jointly and severally', which means attorneys can make decisions on their own or with other attorneys

together: sometimes called 'jointly', which means all the attorneys have to agree on the decision.

A person can also choose to let them make some decisions 'jointly', and others 'jointly and severally'.

Once the CPA or WPA is drawn up and signed, it will still need to be registered at the Scottish Office of the Public Guardian.

Return the completed Power of Attorney and registration form to the Scottish Office of the Public Guardian together with the fee. There are fee exemptions in certain circumstances. Fee payable are:

Submitting of a power of attorney document for registration	Submission of a document conferring a continuing and / or welfare power of attorney under section 19 of the Act.	£81

Deed of Amendment	Registration of a deed of amendment to a continuing or welfare power of attorney under section 19 of the Act.	£81
Duplicate or Replacement Certificate (includes both the Public Guardian's certificate and a bound copy of the power of attorney document)	Provision of a duplicate or replacement certificate issued under section 19(2) of the Act with a copy of the power of attorney document. This only applies to powers of attorney registered manually and not electronically. (Please note that if there are more than 10 pages in the document, an additional 50p per page applies)	£26
Audit of Accounts	Audit of accounts submitted by a continuing attorney under section 20(2)(b) of the Act.	£126

Using a Power of Attorney in Scotland

As soon as a CPA or a WPA has been registered and the documentation received, the attorneys will need to refer to the document to find out when they are to act. It might be at a later date or once an event has taken place. A person may have given their attorneys guidance or a letter to state when they can act.

If someone is caring for someone, to use the a CPA or a WPA, they must show a certified copy of it (not just a photocopy) to any organisation that they want to deal with on their loved one's behalf, including their bank.

If additional certified copies are needed at a later date, any solicitor should be able to do this for a small fee, which they will be able to provide on request. The Scottish Office of the Public Guardian can also provide a duplicate copy for a fee.

If a loved one lacks mental capacity

If a loved one is no longer able to make their own decisions, it's too late to apply for a Continuing Power of Agreement or a Welfare Power of Agreement. In this situation, an application can be made for a 'Guardianship Order' to the appropriate Sheriff Court. Anyone can apply for such an order, including a partner, family member, friend or a professional, such as a solicitor, or someone from the person's local authority social work department.

If successful, the Sheriff can authorise the appointed guardian to do anything that appears necessary or expedient with respect to the property and affairs of the person lacking capacity.

This could be anything to do with their financial affairs including, for example:

- transfer and investment of money
- paying bills
- the sale or purchase of property
- making gifts or wills or the carrying on of a business.

Persons appointed under such orders have to report regularly and are monitored by the appropriate authority in relation to all actions and decisions taken in respect of property and affairs. This supervision is considered appropriate given that an individual who has lost capacity is unable to appoint a person themselves and of their own choosing to act on their behalf.

Further information

The Office of the Public Guardian (Scotland) gives general advice and guidance. Phone 01324 678 398 Monday to Friday, 9am to 5pm.

Call the Age Scotland Helpline on 0800 12 44 222 for advice on power of attorney.

Citizens Advice Bureau's Adviceguide gives guidance on managing affairs for someone else.

Ch.20

Powers of Attorney-Northern Ireland

In Northern Ireland, The Enduring Power of Attorney is used to exercise control over another person affairs.

What is an Enduring power of attorney in Northern Ireland?

An Enduring power of attorney is a legal process in which a person gives the legal right to one or more people, the 'attorneys', to manage their financial affairs and property. This power can come into effect immediately. This means that their attorney(s) can manage part or all of their financial affairs on their behalf, or they can continue to manage them themselves while they are able. Later, if they become unable to deal with their affairs, their attorney(s) can take over.

An EPA has the same status as an Ordinary power of attorney. The difference is that an Ordinary power of attorney becomes invalid if a person becomes unable to manage their finances. An EPA remains effective, provided the necessary steps are taken to register the EPA with the Office of Care and Protection (OCP).

If a person becomes unable to make decisions their self, their attorneys must apply to register the EPA with the OCP. While the registration is being processed, they can use the finances on a persons behalf to pay for essentials, such as food or bills. However, they are not able to arrange larger transactions, such as the sale of a house, until the EPA has been registered.

A person can specify that the EPA can only come into effect once they become unable to manage their affairs. However, there are drawbacks to restricting the EPA in this way. For example, even if a person is not assessed as being mentally incapable, they are likely to find it increasingly difficult to deal with financial affairs as their dementia progresses.

Why should you consider giving Enduring power of attorney?

A person should consider giving somebody Enduring power of attorney (EPA) if they have property, savings, investments or any income apart from benefits. This enables them to select one or more people to act for them now (if they wish), and in the future, should they become unable to make decisions for themselves. Their attorney does not have to be a solicitor; they can appoint a relative or a friend. This option gives them the opportunity to have a say about their future, and it will also make it easier for their carers to act on their behalf in the future.

A person can set up an EPA as long as they are aware of what is involved and can show that they understand the process.

If a person doesn't have an EPA, a controller may have to be appointed to manage their affairs if they become unable to do so. This can be complicated and expensive.

For any queries or complaints about an EPA or controllership (see below) contact the Office of Care and Protection (OCP).

How does a person request a Enduring power of attorney?
First steps
If a person is considering making an EPA it is advisable to seek independent legal advice from a solicitor.

An EPA must be recorded on a specific form, which is available from a solicitor or a stationer specialising in legal documents. Ensure that an up-to-date form is used and that it is completed correctly, or it will not be valid. A solicitor can advise on this. Once the form has been completed, it must be signed by the person involved and witnessed. It must then be signed by the attorney(s) and witnessed. The attorney(s) must sign the form before a person becomes unable to manage their affairs. Attorney(s) may not act as witness(es) for each other's signatures.

If the original document is held by an attorney or lodged with a solicitor or a bank, the person involved should keep a copy for themselves. The solicitor can provide certified copies of the document.

It may help to avoid later misunderstandings if a family conference is called to explain the reasons for making an EPA, so that family can know of the persons wishes.

The attorney's powers

It is important to consider what authority to give an attorney(s). A person can give:

- a general authority, which allows an attorney to carry out any transactions on the persons behalf that they are legally able to delegate
- a limited authority, to deal with certain aspects of property and affairs, as detailed by the person on the EPA form.

Both the general and limited authorities can be qualified by certain conditions or restrictions. A person can also appoint different attorneys to have different responsibilities, although it is advisable to keep arrangements as simple as possible.

The kind of activities an attorney can carry out on a persons behalf include:

- signing cheques and withdrawing money from savings accounts
- buying or selling shares or property
- using your assets to finance a residential or nursing care.

The attorney(s) may also have limited powers to use assets to benefit anyone for whom a person might have been expected to make provision. These circumstances might include buying gifts on special occasions (for example for family or friends on their birthdays), or to continue to make donations to charities that they have donated to in the past. However, an attorney has no power over the person involved. The attorney(s) cannot direct where they live or what medical treatment or care they receive.

The attorney's duties

An attorney is expected to act in the best interests of the person, and to consider the person's needs and wishes as far as possible. They must not take advantage of a persons position to gain any benefit for themselves. They must keep their money and property separate from their own and from that of other people. They should also keep accounts of any dealings on their behalf.

Registering the EPA

When the attorney(s) consider that a person is lacking in capacity or unable to manage their affairs, they should notify the person involved and certain close relatives of their intention to register the

EPA. Notification must be made on an EP1 form. Their solicitor or the OCP can explain which relatives need to be informed.

An application to register must then immediately be made to the OCP on form EP2, accompanied by the original EPA document and the registration fee. Forms EP1 and EP2 are available from legal stationers or free from the OCP.

There is a fee for registration and details of the current fee can be obtained from the OCP. However, the attorney can apply for a reduction if paying this fee is likely to cause hardship. If a person is receiving income support, their care home fees are being paid by the health and social services trust, or their house is their only asset, the fee will generally be waived.

The OCP will hold the papers for 35 days from the date that the last EP1 was sent. This gives the person involved and their relatives time to make any objections. If there are no problems, registration will take place.

Once the EPA has been registered, the attorney(s) can make binding decisions about a persons financial affairs. The OCP can ask attorneys to produce accounts for them to check, although this usually only occurs if there has been a query or complaint about the way the EPA is being handled. There is a charge for checking accounts.

Complaints

Attorneys are expected to act 'reasonably' and in a persons best interests. The OCP does not monitor the way an attorney acts under the EPA. However, they will consider any complaints about the way an attorney acts once the EPA has been registered. The OCP will decide whether that person should remain an attorney or whether other arrangements should be made.

Controllership

If a person has not made an EPA and they become unable to manage their affairs, it may be necessary to appoint a controller to manage them on their behalf. Appointing a controller is done through the Office of Care and Protection (OCP). However, if managing their financial affairs consists simply of managing their income from benefits, it may be done through appointeeship.

Who can become a controller?

A close relative usually acts as a controller, but it could be a friend or a solicitor. If nobody suitable can be found, the OCP can appoint the official solicitor to act as a controller. A controller has a considerable number of responsibilities that can be very demanding and time-consuming. Anyone wishing to become a controller should consider whether they will be able to fulfil the obligations. They should read the free booklets produced by the OCP to ensure that they understand what being a controller involves.

What can a controller do?

The controller will manage a persons income to ensure that their day-to-day needs are met and bills are paid. They will also ensure that any property is kept in a good state, income tax affairs are kept up to date and important documents are in order and kept safely.

The OCP must authorise any use of capital, such as the home or other property, on the persons behalf. The controller must liaise with the OCP about any investments, which are usually made by the OCP, and about the sale of property, which must be approved by the OCP.

The controller should be aware of a persons needs and wishes and consult them as far as possible on how they would like their money to be spent. A controller has to submit annual accounts to the OCP and take out a security bond to safeguard assets. They can reclaim the cost from the persons money.

How does a person become a controller?

The first step is to get the application forms from the OCP. The OCP can also help with queries about the forms, although it cannot give legal advice. The person filling in the forms can apply to be appointed as controller themselves or ask for someone else to be appointed. The completed forms should be returned to the OCP with the application fee.

If the court is satisfied that this is the right course of action, the OCP will appoint a controller (or make a short procedure order, see below). Both these arrangements give the person selected the legal authority to manage a persons financial affairs on their behalf, in accordance with the court's instructions. In either case, the court will set out the exact duties and responsibilities involved.

Fees

There are a number of fees applicable. The OCP can give details of these.

Short procedure order

In some cases the OCP may decide to make a 'short procedure order', rather than appointing a controller. This is a simpler and more limited arrangement. It usually occurs where the value of someone's assets or income is relatively low. It can also occur when there is no property to be sold and a person does not have a level of income that the court considers in need of being managed by a controller. A short procedure order may authorise someone to:

- use pensions and income on behalf of a person
- use social security benefits and money held in a bank or building society
- pay care home fees and any other debts and expenses
- make sure any documents and valuables are safely looked after.

For full details of the criteria for a short procedure order contact the OCP.

****

Useful organisations

Northern Ireland

Age NI

3 wer Crescent

Belfast BT7 1NR

T 0808 808 7575

E info@ageni.org

W www.ageuk.org.uk/northern-ireland

Provides information and advice for older people in Northern Ireland.

Office of Care and Protection

Room 2.2A, Second Floor

Royal Courts of Justice

Chichester Street

Belfast BT1 3JF

T 0300 20 7802

The Office of Care and Protection is part of the family division of the high court and is the administration office that deals with the registration of EPAs and the appointment of controllers.

The Law Centre NI

2-4 Queen Street.

Belfast. BT1 6ED.

Phone: 028 9024 4401.
Fax: 028 9023 6340.
Email: admin@lawcentreni.org.

Western Area Office

9 Clarendon Street

Londonerry BT48 7EP

T 028 7126 2433

E admin.derry@lawcentreniwest.org

The Law Centre provides a legal service in specific areas of law to people on low incomes who live or work in Northern Ireland.

Useful contacts generally

Age UK-England

Age UK,

Tavis House,

1-6 Tavistock Square,

London WC1H 9NA.

0800 169 8787

E contact@ageuk.org.uk

www.ageuk.org.uk

Age UK Wales

Age Cymru,

Ground Floor,

Mariners House,

Trident Court,

East Moors Road,

Cardiff, CF24 5TD

08000 223 444

www.ageuk.org.uk/cymru

Age UK-Scotland

Age Scotland,

Causewayside House,

160 Causewayside,

Edinburgh EH9 1PR

0800 12 44 222

https://www.ageuk.org.uk/scotland

Age UK Northern Ireland

Age NI,

3 Lower Crescent,

Belfast

BT7 1NR

0808 808 7575

www.ageuk.org.uk/northern-ireland

The Age UK network includes Age Scotland, Age Cymru and Age NI and more than 150 local Age UKs throughout England. Together, we provide a wide range of services to help people in later life throughout the UK.

Alzheimer's Society

43-44 Crutched Friars

London

EC3N 2AE

0330 333 0804

www.alzheimers.org.uk

Citizens Advice Bureau (CAB)

To find details of your nearest CAB look in the phone book, ask at your local library or consult the CAB website at www.citizensadvice.org.uk

Your local CAB is often the best starting point for advice. The service is free, confidential and independent. Most CABs have a solicitor and some have an accountant available at certain times to give free initial advice.

Court of Protection

Court of Protection

PO Box 70185

First Avenue House

42-49 High Holborn

London

WC1A 9JA

Email courtofprotectionenquiries.gsi.gov.uk

Enquiries 0300 456 4600

The Court of Protection is a specialist court for all issues relating to people who lack capacity to make specific decisions.

Office of the Public Guardian

102 Petty France

London

SWEH 9AJ

T 020 3334 3555

E customerservices@publicguardian.gsi.gov.uk

W www.direct.gov.uk/mentalcapacity

Customer services provide free booklets on Enduring Power of Attorney, Lasting Power of Attorney and deputyship. Their phoneline is available from 9am to 5pm on weekdays.

Solicitors for the Elderly

Sue Carraturo

Solicitors for the Elderly Ltd

Room 17, Conbar House

Mead Lane

Hertford SG13 7AP

T 0844 5676 173

E admin@solicitorsfortheelderly.com

****

Glossary of terms

Ability to make decisions-the donor can carry on making decisions providing he or she has the capacity to do so.

Duties of the Attorney-Statutory duties to act in accordance with the principles of the Mental Health Act best interest and with regard to the guidance of the code of practice.

Joint and Several Attorneys-where two or more persons are appointed and they must either act jointly or jointly and severally.

Lasting Power of Attorney-must be in the prescribed form.

Notification-the names of the person the donor wishes to be notified of any Application to register or must contain a Statement that there are no such persons.

Objection to Registration-the donor, the Attorney and the named person may object if the EPA is not valid or it no longer exists if the Attorneys have behaved badly.

Property and Financial Affairs
Registering the Power-Registration can take place before the donor has lost capacity.

Registration-the Attorney cannot act under the LPA until it is registered with the Public Guardian.

Revoking the power-the donor may revoke the LPA and it may come to an end on the dissolution or annulment of marriage or civil partnership unless the instrument provider will not do so.

The Certificate provider-this is a person of the prescribed description who ensures that the donor understands the purpose of the instrument and the scope of the authority.

The Public Guardian-the office with whom the documentation needs to be registered. There are two types of Lasting Powers of Attorney:

Personal Welfare including giving or refusing consent to treatment. This can only be used when the donor lacks capacity.

****

Index

Appendix

Form 1. LP1F Registering a Financial Lasting Powers of Attorney

Form 2. LP1H Regsitering a Health and Care PLA

Form 3. LP3 Form for notifying people of Registering an LPA

A very useful guide to the overall process of powers of attorney can be obtained from www.gov.uk/power-of-attorney, as can the above forms.

Office of the
Public Guardian

Lasting power
of attorney

Financial decisions

**Registering
an LPA costs**

£82

This fee is means-tested:
see the application
Guide part B

Use this for:

- running your bank and savings accounts
- making or selling investments
- paying your bills
- buying or selling your house

How to complete this form

PLEASE WRITE IN CAPITAL LETTERS USING A BLACK PEN

☒ Mark your choice with an X

■ If you make a mistake, fill in the box and then mark the correct
choice with an X

Don't use correction fluid. Cross out mistakes and rewrite nearby.
Everyone involved in each section must initial each change.

Making an LPA online is simpler, clearer and faster

Our smart online form gives you just the right amount of help
exactly when you need it: **www.gov.uk/power-of-attorney**

— Before
you start...

This form is also available in Welsh. Call the helpline on 0300 456 0300.

The people involved in your LPA

You'll find it easier to make an LPA if you first choose the people you want to help you. **Note their names here now** so you can refer back later.

People you must have to make an LPA

Donor

[ ]

If you are filling this form in for yourself, you are the donor. If you are filling this in for a friend or relative, they are the donor.

Attorneys

[ ]

Attorneys are the people you pick to make decisions for you. They don't need legal training.

They should be people you trust and know well; for example, your husband, wife, partner, adult children or good friends.

Choose one attorney or more. If you have a lot, they might find it hard to make decisions together.

Certificate provider

[ ]

You need someone to confirm that no one is forcing you to make an LPA and you understand what you are doing. This is your 'certificate provider'. They must either:

• have relevant professional skills, such as a doctor or lawyer
• have known you well for at least two years, such as a friend or colleague

Some people can't be a certificate provider. See the list in the Guide, part A10.

Witnesses

[ ]

You can't witness your attorneys' signatures and they can't witness yours. Anyone else over 18 years old can be a witness.

People you might want to include in your LPA

Replacement attorneys

[ ]

You don't have to appoint replacement attorneys but they help protect your LPA. Without them, your LPA might not work if one of your original attorneys stops acting for you.

People to notify

[ ]

'People to notify' add security. They can raise concerns about your LPA before it's registered – for example, if they think you are under pressure to make the LPA.

This page is not part of the form

Lasting power of attorney for property and financial affairs

Section 1
The donor

You are appointing other people to make decisions on your behalf.
You are 'the donor'.

Restrictions – you must be at least 18 years old and be able to understand
and make decisions for yourself (called 'mental capacity').

Help?

For help with
this section,
see the
Guide, part A1.

**If you are filling this in for
a friend or relative** and
they can no longer make
decisions independently,
they can't make an LPA.
See the Guide 'Before you
start' for more information.

Title

First names

Last name

Any other names you're known by (optional – eg your married name)

Date of birth

Day   Month   Year

Address

Postcode

Email address (optional)

For OPG office use only

LPA registration date

OPG reference number

Day   Month   Year

Only valid with the official stamp here.

LP1F Property and financial
affairs (07.15)

1

Section 2
The attorneys

The people you choose to make decisions for you are called your 'attorneys'. Your attorneys don't need special legal knowledge or training. They should be people you trust and know well. Common choices include your husband, wife or partner, son or daughter, or your best friend.

You need at least one attorney, but you can have more.

You'll also be able to choose 'replacement attorneys' in section 4. They can step in if one of the attorneys you appoint here can no longer act for you.

To appoint a trust corporation, fill in the first attorney space and tick the box in that section. They must sign Continuation sheet 4. For more about trust corporations, see the Guide, part A2.

Restrictions – Attorneys must be at least 18 years old and must have mental capacity to make decisions. They must not be bankrupt or subject to a debt relief order.

Help?

For help with this section, see the Guide, part A2.

Title	First names

Last name (or trust corporation name)

Date of birth

Day	Month	Year

Address

Postcode

Email address (optional)

☐ This attorney is a trust corporation.

Title	First names

Last name

Date of birth

Day	Month	Year

Address

Postcode

Email address (optional)

Section 2 – continued

Title	First names		Title	First names

Last name

Date of birth

Day   Month   Year

Address

Postcode

Email address (optional)

Last name

Date of birth

Day   Month   Year

Address

Postcode

Email address (optional)

☐ **More attorneys** – I want to appoint more than 4 attorneys. Use Continuation sheet 1.

Section 3
How should your attorneys make decisions?

You need to choose whether your attorneys can make decisions on their own or must agree some or all decisions unanimously.

Whatever you choose, they must always act in your best interests.

☐ **I only appointed one attorney** (turn to section 4)

How do you want your attorneys to work together? (tick one only)

☐ **Jointly and severally**
Attorneys can make decisions on their own or together. Most people choose this option because it's the most practical. Attorneys can get together to make important decisions if they wish, but can make simple or urgent decisions on their own. It's up to the attorneys to choose when they act together or alone. It also means that if one of the attorneys dies or can no longer act, your LPA will still work.

If one attorney makes a decision, it has the same effect as if all the attorneys made that decision.

☐ **Jointly**
Attorneys must agree unanimously on every decision, however big or small. Remember, some simple decisions could be delayed because it takes time to get the attorneys together. If your attorneys can't agree a decision, then they can only make that decision by going to court.

Be careful – if one attorney dies or can no longer act, all your attorneys become unable to act. This is because the law says a group appointed 'jointly' is a single unit. Your LPA will stop working unless you appoint at least one replacement attorney (in section 4).

☐ **Jointly for some decisions, jointly and severally for other decisions**
Attorneys must agree unanimously on some decisions, but can make others on their own. If you choose this option, you must list the decisions your attorneys should make jointly and agree unanimously on Continuation sheet 2. The wording you use is important. There are examples in the Guide, part A3.

Be careful – if one attorney dies or can no longer act, none of your attorneys will be able to make any of the decisions you've said should be made jointly. Your LPA will stop working for those decisions unless you appoint at least one replacement attorney (in section 4). Your original attorneys will still be able to make any of the other decisions alongside your replacement attorneys.

Help?
For help with this section, see the Guide, part A3.

If you choose 'jointly for some decisions...', you may want to take legal advice, particularly if the examples in part A3 of the the Guide, don't match your needs.

Only valid with the official stamp here.

LP1F Property and financial affairs (07.15)

4

Section 4
Replacement attorneys

This section is optional, but we recommend you consider it

Replacement attorneys are a backup in case one of your original attorneys can't make decisions for you any more.

To appoint a trust corporation, fill in the first attorney space below and tick the box in that section. They must sign Continuation sheet 4.

Reasons replacement attorneys step in – if one of your original attorneys dies, loses capacity, no longer wants to be your attorney, becomes bankrupt or subject to a debt relief order or is no longer legally your husband, wife or civil partner.

Restrictions – replacement attorneys must be at least 18 years old and have mental capacity to make decisions. They must not be bankrupt or subject to a debt relief order.

Help?

For help with this section, see the Guide, part A4.

Title	First names

Last name   (or trust corporation name)

Date of birth

Day   Month   Year

Address

Postcode

☐ This attorney is a trust corporation.

Title	First names

Last name

Date of birth

Day   Month   Year

Address

Postcode

☐ **More replacements** – I want to appoint more than two replacements. Use Continuation sheet 1.

When and how your replacement attorneys can act

Replacement attorneys usually step in when one of your **original** attorneys stops acting for you. If there's more than one **replacement** attorney, they will all step in at once. If they **fully** replace your original attorney(s) at once, they will usually act jointly. You can change some aspects of this, but most people don't. See the Guide, part A4.

You should consider taking legal advice if you want to change when or how your replacement attorneys act.

☐ I want to change when or how my attorneys can act (optional). Use Continuation sheet 2.

Only valid with the official stamp here.

LP1F Property and financial affairs (07.15)

5

Section 5
When can your attorneys make decisions?

You can allow your attorneys to make decisions:
• as soon as the LPA has been registered by the Office of the Public Guardian
• only when you don't have mental capacity

While you have mental capacity you will be in control of all decisions affecting you. If you choose the first option, your attorneys can only make decisions on your behalf if you allow them to. They are responsible to you for any decisions you let them make.

Your attorneys must always act in your best interests.

Help?

For help with this section, see the Guide, part A5.

When do you want your attorneys to be able to make decisions?
(mark one only)

☐ **As soon as my LPA has been registered**
(and also when I don't have mental capacity)

Most people choose this option because it is the most practical.

While you still have mental capacity, your attorneys can only act **with your consent**. If you later lose capacity, they can continue to act on your behalf for all decisions covered by this LPA.

This option is useful if you are able to make your own decisions but there's another reason you want your attorneys to help you – for example, if you're away on holiday, or if you have a physical condition that makes it difficult to visit the bank, talk on the phone or sign documents.

☐ **Only when I don't have mental capacity**

Be careful – this can make your LPA a lot less useful. Your attorneys might be asked to prove you do not have mental capacity each time they try to use this LPA.

Section 6
People to notify when the LPA is registered

This section is optional

You can let people know that you're going to register your LPA. They can raise any concerns they have about the LPA – for example, if there was any pressure or fraud in making it.

When the LPA is registered, the person applying to register (you or one of your attorneys) must send a notice to each 'person to notify'.

You can't put your attorneys or replacement attorneys here.

People to notify can object to the LPA, but only for certain reasons (listed in the notification form LP3). After that, they are no longer involved in the LPA. Choose people who care about your best interests and who would be willing to speak up if they were concerned.

Help?

For help with this section, see the Guide, part A6.

Title | First names

Last name

Address

Postcode

Title | First names

Last name

Address

Postcode

Title | First names

Last name

Address

Postcode

Title | First names

Last name

Address

Postcode

☐ I want to appoint another person to notify (maximum is 5) – use Continuation sheet 1.

Only valid with the official stamp here.

LP1F Property and financial affairs (07.15)

Section 7
Preferences and instructions

This section is optional

You can tell your attorneys how you'd **prefer** them to make decisions, or give them specific **instructions** which they must follow when making decisions.

Most people leave this page blank – you can just talk to your attorneys so they understand how you want them to make decisions for you.

Preferences

Your attorneys don't have to follow your preferences but they should keep them in mind. For examples of preferences, see the Guide, part A7.

Help?

For help with this section, see the Guide, part A7.

Preferences – use words like 'prefer' and 'would like'

☐ I need more space – use Continuation sheet 2.

Instructions

Your attorneys will have to follow your instructions exactly. For examples of instructions, see the Guide, part A7.

Be careful – if you give instructions that are not legally correct they would have to be removed before your LPA could be registered.

 If you want to give instructions, you may want to take legal advice.

Instructions – use words like 'must' and 'have to'

☐ I need more space – use Continuation sheet 2.

Only valid with the official stamp here.

Section 8
Your legal rights and responsibilities

 Everyone signing the LPA must read this information

In sections 9 to 11, you, the certificate provider, all your attorneys and your replacement attorneys must sign this lasting power of attorney to form a legal agreement between you (a deed).

By signing this lasting power of attorney, you (the donor) are appointing people (attorneys) to make decisions for you.

LPAs are governed by the Mental Capacity Act 2005 (MCA), regulations made under it and the MCA Code of Practice. Attorneys must have regard to these documents. The Code of Practice is available from www.gov.uk/opg/mca-code or from The Stationery Office.

Help?

For help with this section, see the Guide, part A8.

Your attorneys must follow the principles of the Mental Capacity Act:

1. Your attorneys must assume that you can make your own decisions unless it is established that you cannot do so.
2. Your attorneys must help you to make as many of your own decisions as you can. They must take all practical steps to help you to make a decision. They can only treat you as unable to make a decision if they have not succeeded in helping you make a decision through those steps.
3. Your attorneys must not treat you as unable to make a decision simply because you make an unwise decision.
4. Your attorneys must act and make decisions in your best interests when you are unable to make a decision.
5. Before your attorneys make a decision or act for you, they must consider whether they can make the decision or act in a way that is less restrictive of your rights and freedom but still achieves the purpose.

Your attorneys must always act in your best interests. This is explained in the Application guide, part A8, and defined in the MCA Code of Practice.

Before this LPA can be used:
• it must be registered by the Office of the Public Guardian (OPG)
• it may be limited to when you don't have mental capacity, according to your choice in section 5

Cancelling your LPA: You can cancel this LPA at any time, as long as you have mental capacity to do so. It doesn't matter if the LPA has been registered or not. For more information, see the Guide, part D.

Your will and your LPA: Your attorneys cannot use this LPA to change your will. This LPA will expire when you die. Your attorneys must then send the registered LPA, any certified copies and a copy of your death certificate to the Office of the Public Guardian.

Data protection: For information about how OPG uses your personal data, see the Guide, part D.

Section 9
Signature: donor

By signing on this page I confirm all of the following:

- I have read this lasting power of attorney (LPA) including section 8 'Your legal rights and responsibilities', or I have had it read to me

- I appoint and give my attorneys authority to make decisions about my property and financial affairs, including when I cannot act for myself because I lack mental capacity, subject to the terms of this LPA and to the provisions of the Mental Capacity Act 2005

- I have either appointed people to notify (in section 6) or I have chosen not to notify anyone when the LPA is registered

- I agree to the information I've provided being used by the Office of the Public Guardian in carrying out its duties

Be careful

Sign this page (and any continuation sheets) before anyone signs sections 10 and 11.

Donor	Witness
Signed (or marked) by the person giving this lasting power of attorney and delivered as a deed.	The witness must not be an attorney or replacement attorney appointed under this LPA, and must be aged 18 or over.
Signature or mark	**Signature or mark**
Date signed or marked	**Full name of witness**
Day Month Year	
If you have used Continuation sheets 1 or 2 you must sign and date each continuation sheet at the same time as you sign this page.	**Address**
If you can't sign this LPA you can make a mark instead. If you can't sign or make a mark you can instruct someone else to sign for you, using Continuation sheet 3.	Postcode

Help? For help with this section, see the Guide, part A9.

Only valid with the official stamp here.

! **Only sign this section after the donor has signed section 9**

The 'certificate provider' signs to confirm they've discussed the lasting power of attorney (LPA) with the donor, that the donor understands what they're doing and that nobody is forcing them to do it. The 'certificate provider' should be either:

 Help?

For help with this section, see the Guide, part A10.

- someone who has known the donor personally for at least 2 years, such as a friend, neighbour, colleague or former colleague
- someone with relevant professional skills, such as the donor's GP, a healthcare professional or a solicitor

A certificate provider **can't** be one of the attorneys.

Certificate provider's statement

I certify that, as far as I'm aware, at the time of signing section 9:

- the donor understood the purpose of this LPA and the scope of the authority conferred under it
- no fraud or undue pressure is being used to induce the donor to create this LPA
- there is nothing else which would prevent this LPA from being created by the completion of this instrument

By signing this section I confirm that:

- I am aged 18 or over
- I have read this LPA, including section 8 'Your legal rights and responsibilities'
- there is no restriction on my acting as a certificate provider
- the donor has chosen me as someone who has known them personally for at least 2 years **OR**
- the donor has chosen me as a person with relevant professional skills and expertise

Restrictions – the certificate provider must not be:

- an attorney or replacement attorney named in this LPA or any other LPA or enduring power of attorney for the donor
- a member of the donor's family or of one of the attorneys' families, including husbands, wives, civil partners, in-laws and step-relatives
- an unmarried partner, boyfriend or girlfriend of either the donor or one of the attorneys (whether or not they live at the same address)
- the donor's or an attorney's business partner
- the donor's or an attorney's employee
- an owner, manager, director or employee of a care home where the donor lives

Certificate provider

Title

First names

Last name

Address

Postcode

Signature or mark

Date signed or marked

Day   Month   Year

Only valid with the official stamp here.

Section 11
Signature: attorney or replacement

 Only sign this section after the certificate provider has signed section 10

All the attorneys and replacement attorneys need to sign.
There are 4 copies of this page – make more copies if you need to.

By signing this section I understand and confirm all of the following:

- I am aged 18 or over
- I have read this lasting power of attorney (LPA) including section 8 'Your legal rights and responsibilities', or I have had it read to me
- I have a duty to act based on the principles of the Mental Capacity Act 2005 and to have regard to the Mental Capacity Act Code of Practice
- I must make decisions and act in the best interests of the donor
- I must take into account any instructions or preferences set out in this LPA
- I can make decisions and act only when this LPA has been registered and at the time indicated in section 5 of this LPA

Further statement by a replacement attorney: I understand that I have the authority to act under this LPA only after an original attorney's appointment is terminated. I must notify the Public Guardian if this happens.

Help?

For help with this section, see the Guide, part A11.

Attorney or replacement attorney	Witness
Signed (or marked) by the attorney or replacement attorney and delivered as a deed.	The witness must not be the donor of this LPA, and must be aged 18 or over.
Signature or mark	Signature or mark
Date signed or marked	Full names of witness
Day Month Year	
Title First names	Address
Last name	
	Postcode

Section 11
Signature: attorney or replacement

 Only sign this section after the certificate provider has signed section 10

All the attorneys and replacement attorneys need to sign.
There are 4 copies of this page – make more copies if you need to.

By signing this section I understand and confirm all of the following:

- I am aged 18 or over
- I have read this lasting power of attorney (LPA) including section 8 'Your legal rights and responsibilities', or I have had it read to me
- I have a duty to act based on the principles of the Mental Capacity Act 2005 and to have regard to the Mental Capacity Act Code of Practice
- I must make decisions and act in the best interests of the donor
- I must take into account any instructions or preferences set out in this LPA
- I can make decisions and act only when this LPA has been registered and at the time indicated in section 5 of this LPA

Further statement by a replacement attorney: I understand that I have the authority to act under this LPA only after an original attorney's appointment is terminated. I must notify the Public Guardian if this happens.

Help?

For help with this section, see the Guide, part A11.

Attorney or replacement attorney	Witness
Signed (or marked) by the attorney or replacement attorney and delivered as a deed.	The witness must not be the donor of this LPA, and must be aged 18 or over.
Signature or mark	Signature or mark
Date signed or marked	
Day Month Year	Full names of witness
Title First names	
	Address
Last name	
	Postcode

Section 11
Signature: attorney or replacement

 Only sign this section after the certificate provider has signed section 10

All the attorneys and replacement attorneys need to sign.
There are 4 copies of this page – make more copies if you need to.

Help?

For help with this section, see the Guide, part A11.

By signing this section I understand and confirm all of the following:

• I am aged 18 or over

• I have read this lasting power of attorney (LPA) including section 8 'Your legal rights and responsibilities', or I have had it read to me

• I have a duty to act based on the principles of the Mental Capacity Act 2005 and to have regard to the Mental Capacity Act Code of Practice

• I must make decisions and act in the best interests of the donor

• I must take into account any instructions or preferences set out in this LPA

• I can make decisions and act only when this LPA has been registered and at the time indicated in section 5 of this LPA

Further statement by a replacement attorney: I understand that I have the authority to act under this LPA only after an original attorney's appointment is terminated. I must notify the Public Guardian if this happens.

Attorney or replacement attorney	Witness
Signed (or marked) by the attorney or replacement attorney and delivered as a deed.	The witness must not be the donor of this LPA, and must be aged 18 or over.
Signature or mark	Signature or mark
Date signed or marked	Full names of witness
Day Month Year	
Title First names	Address
Last name	
	Postcode

Section 11
Signature: attorney or replacement

 Only sign this section after the certificate provider has signed section 10

All the attorneys and replacement attorneys need to sign.
There are 4 copies of this page – make more copies if you need to.

By signing this section I understand and confirm all of the following:

- I am aged 18 or over
- I have read this lasting power of attorney (LPA) including section 8 'Your legal rights and responsibilities', or I have had it read to me
- I have a duty to act based on the principles of the Mental Capacity Act 2005 and to have regard to the Mental Capacity Act Code of Practice
- I must make decisions and act in the best interests of the donor
- I must take into account any instructions or preferences set out in this LPA
- I can make decisions and act only when this LPA has been registered and at the time indicated in section 5 of this LPA

Further statement by a replacement attorney: I understand that I have the authority to act under this LPA only after an original attorney's appointment is terminated. I must notify the Public Guardian if this happens.

Help?

For help with this section, see the Guide, part A11.

Attorney or replacement attorney	Witness
Signed (or marked) by the attorney or replacement attorney and delivered as a deed.	The witness must not be the donor of this LPA, and must be aged 18 or over.

Attorney or replacement attorney

Signature or mark

Date signed or marked

Day   Month   Year

Title   First names

Last name

Witness

Signature or mark

Full names of witness

Address

Postcode

Only valid with the official stamp here.

Now register your LPA

Before the LPA can be used, it **must** be registered by the Office of the Public Guardian (OPG). Continue filling in this form to register the LPA. See part B of the Guide.

People to notify

If there are any 'people to notify' listed in section 6, you must notify them that you are registering the LPA now. See part C of the Guide.

Fill in and send each of them a copy of the form to notify people – LP3.

When you sign section 15 of this form, you are confirming that you've sent forms to the 'people to notify'.

Register now

You do not have to register immediately, but it's a good idea in case you've made any mistakes. If you delay until after the donor loses mental capacity, it will be impossible to fix any errors. This could make the whole LPA invalid and it will not be possible to register or use it.

Register your lasting power of attorney

Section 12
The applicant

You can only apply to register if you are either the donor or attorney(s) for this LPA. The donor and attorney(s) should not apply together.

Who is applying to register the LPA? (tick one only)

☐ **Donor** – the donor needs to sign section 15

☐ **Attorney(s)** – If the attorneys were appointed jointly (in section 3) then they **all** need to sign section 15. Otherwise, only one of the attorneys needs to sign

Help?

For help with this section, see the Guide, part B2.

Write the name and date of birth for each attorney that is applying to register the LPA. Don't include any attorneys who are not applying.

Title	First names

Last name

Date of birth

Day Month Year

Title	First names

Last name

Date of birth

Day Month Year

Title	First names

Last name

Date of birth

Day Month Year

Title	First names

Last name

Date of birth

Day Month Year

Section 13
Who do you want to receive the LPA?

We need to know who to send the LPA to once it is registered. We might also need to contact someone with questions about the application.

We already have the addresses of the donor and attorneys, so you don't have to repeat any of those here, unless they have changed.

Who would you like to receive the LPA and any correspondence?

☐ **The donor**

☐ **An attorney** (write name below)

☐ **Other** (write name and address below)

Title

First names

Last name

Company (optional)

Address

Postcode

How would the person above prefer to be contacted?

You can choose more than one.

☐ **Post**

☐ **Phone**

☐ **Email**

☐ **Welsh** (we will write to the person in Welsh)

Help?

For help with this section, see the Guide, part B3.

Section 14
Application fee

There's a fee for registering a lasting power of attorney – the amount is shown on the cover sheet of this form or on form LPA120.

The fee changes from time to time. You can check you are paying the correct amount at www.gov.uk/power-of-attorney/how-much-it-costs or call 0300 456 0300. The Office of the Public Guardian can't register your LPA until you have paid the fee.

How would you like to pay?

☐ **Card** For security, **don't** write your credit or debit card details here. We'll contact you to process the payment.

Your phone number

☐ **Cheque** Enclose a cheque with your application.

Help?

For help with this section, see the Guide, part B4.

Reduced application fee

If the donor has a low income, you may not have to pay the full amount. See the Guide, part B4 for details.

☐ **I want to apply to pay a reduced fee**

You'll need to fill in form LPA120 and include it with your application. You'll also **need to send proof** that the donor is eligible to pay a reduced fee.

Are you making a repeat application?

If you've already applied to register an LPA and the Office of the Public Guardian said that it was not possible to register it, you can apply again within 3 months and pay a reduced fee.

☐ **I'm making a repeat application**

Case number

For OPG office use only

Payment reference

Payment date

Day	Month	Year

Amount

Section 15
Signature

 Do not sign this section until after sections 9, 10 and 11 have been signed.

The person applying to register the LPA (see section 12) must sign and date this section. This is either the donor or attorney(s) but not both together.

If the **attorneys** are applying to register the LPA and they were appointed to act **jointly** (in section 3), they must all sign.

By signing this section I confirm the following:

- I apply to register the LPA that accompanies this application
- I have informed 'people to notify' named in section 6 of the LPA (if any) of my intention to register the LPA
- I certify that the information in this form is correct to the best of my knowledge and belief

 Help?

For help with this section, see the Guide, part B5.

Signature or mark	Signature or mark

Date signed	Date signed
Day Month Year	Day Month Year

Signature or mark	Signature or mark

Date signed	Date signed
Day Month Year	Day Month Year

If more than 4 attorneys need to sign, make copies of this page.

Check your lasting power of attorney

You don't have to use this checklist, but it'll help you make sure you've completed your LPA correctly.

☐ The donor filled in sections 1 to 7.

☐ The donor signed section 9 in the presence of a witness. The donor also signed any copies of continuation sheets 1 and 2 that were used, on the same date as signing section 9.

☐ The certificate provider signed section 10.

☐ All the attorneys and replacement attorneys signed section 11, in the presence of witness(es).

☐ Sections 9, 10 and 11 were signed in order. Section 9 must have been signed first, then section 10, then section 11. They can be dated the same day or different days.

☐ The donor or an attorney completed sections 12 to 15. If the attorneys are applying and were appointed 'jointly' (section 3), they have all signed section 15 of this form.

☐ I've paid the application fee or applied for a reduced fee. If I've applied for a reduced fee, I've included the required evidence and completed form LPA120A.

☐ If there were any people to notify in section 6, I've notified them using form LP3.

☐ I've not left out any of the pages of the LPA, even the ones where I didn't write anything or there were no boxes to fill in.

Helpline
0300 456 0300 📞

Send to:

Office of the Public Guardian
PO Box 16185
Birmingham B2 2WH

LP1F Property and financial affairs (03.17)

Office of the
Public Guardian

Lasting power
of attorney

Health and care
decisions

Registering
an LPA costs

£82

This fee is means-tested:
see the application
Guide part B

Use this for:

- the type of health care and medical treatment you
  receive, including life-sustaining treatment
- where you live
- day-to-day matters such as your diet and daily routine

How to complete this form

PLEASE WRITE IN CAPITAL LETTERS USING A BLACK PEN

 Mark your choice with an X

■ If you make a mistake, fill in the box and then mark the correct
choice with an X

Don't use correction fluid. Cross out mistakes and rewrite nearby.
Everyone involved in each section must initial each change.

Making an LPA online is simpler, clearer and faster

Our smart online form gives you just the right amount of help
exactly when you need it: **www.gov.uk/power-of-attorney**

**Before
you start...**

This form is also available in Welsh. Call the helpline on 0300 456 0300.

The people involved in your LPA

 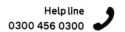

You'll find it easier to make an LPA if you first choose the people you want to help you. **Note their names here now** so you can refer back later.

People you must have to make an LPA

Donor

If you are filling this form in for yourself, you are the donor. If you are filling this in for a friend or relative, they are the donor.

Attorneys

Attorneys are the people you pick to make decisions for you. They don't need legal training.

They should be people you trust and know well; for example, your husband, wife, partner, adult children or good friends.

Choose one attorney or more. If you have a lot, they might find it hard to make decisions together.

Certificate provider

You need someone to confirm that no one is forcing you to make an LPA and you understand what you are doing. This is your 'certificate provider'. They must either:

- have relevant professional skills, such as a doctor or lawyer
- have known you well for at least two years, such as a friend or colleague

Some people can't be a certificate provider. See the list in the Guide, part A10.

Witnesses

You can't witness your attorneys' signatures and they can't witness yours. Anyone else over 18 years old can be a witness.

People you might want to include in your LPA

Replacement attorneys

You don't have to appoint replacement attorneys but they help protect your LPA. Without them, your LPA might not work if one of your original attorneys stops acting for you.

People to notify

'People to notify' add security. They can raise concerns about your LPA before it's registered – for example, if they think you are under pressure to make the LPA.

Office of the Public Guardian

Lasting power of attorney for health and welfare

Section 1
The donor

You are appointing other people to make decisions on your behalf.
You are 'the donor'.

Restrictions – you must be at least 18 years old and be able to understand and make decisions for yourself (called 'mental capacity').

Title   First names

Last name

Any other names you're known by (optional – eg your married name)

Date of birth

Day   Month   Year

Address

Postcode

Email address (optional)

Help?

For help with this section, see the Guide, part A1.

If you are filling this in for a friend or relative and they can no longer make decisions independently, they can't make an LPA. See the Guide 'Before you start' for more information.

For OPG office use only

LPA registration date

Day   Month   Year

OPG reference number

Only valid with the official stamp here.

Section 2
The attorneys

The people you choose to make decisions for you are called your 'attorneys'. Your attorneys don't need special legal knowledge or training. They should be people you trust and know well. Common choices include your husband, wife or partner, son or daughter, or your best friend.

You need at least one attorney, but you can have more.

You'll also be able to choose 'replacement attorneys' in section 4. They can step in if one of the attorneys you appoint here can no longer act for you.

Restrictions – Attorneys must be at least 18 years old and must have mental capacity to make decisions.

Help?

For help with this section, see the Guide, part A2.

Title	First names		Title	First names

Last name

Last name

Date of birth

Day   Month   Year

Date of birth

Day   Month   Year

Address

Postcode

Address

Postcode

Email address (optional)

Email address (optional)

Title First names

Last name

Date of birth

Day Month Year

Address

Postcode

Email address (optional)

Title First names

Last name

Date of birth

Day Month Year

Address

Postcode

Email address (optional)

More attorneys – I want to appoint more than 4 attorneys. Use Continuation sheet 1.

Section 3
How should your attorneys make decisions?

You need to choose whether your attorneys can make decisions on their own or must agree some or all decisions unanimously.

Whatever you choose, they must always act in your best interests.

☐ **I only appointed one attorney** (turn to section 4)

How do you want your attorneys to work together? (tick one only)

☐ **Jointly and severally**

Attorneys can make decisions on their own or together. Most people choose this option because it's the most practical. Attorneys can get together to make important decisions if they wish, but can make simple or urgent decisions on their own. It's up to the attorneys to choose when they act together or alone. It also means that if one of the attorneys dies or can no longer act, your LPA will still work.

If one attorney makes a decision, it has the same effect as if all the attorneys made that decision.

☐ **Jointly**

Attorneys must agree unanimously on every decision, however big or small. Remember, some simple decisions could be delayed because it takes time to get the attorneys together. If your attorneys can't agree a decision, then they can only make that decision by going to court.

Be careful – if one attorney dies or can no longer act, all your attorneys become unable to act. This is because the law says a group appointed 'jointly' is a single unit. Your LPA will stop working unless you appoint at least one replacement attorney (in section 4).

☐ **Jointly for some decisions, jointly and severally for other decisions**

Attorneys must agree unanimously on some decisions, but can make others on their own. If you choose this option, you must list the decisions your attorneys should make jointly and agree unanimously on Continuation sheet 2. The wording you use is important. There are examples in the Guide, part A3.

Be careful – if one of your attorneys dies or can no longer act, none of your attorneys will be able to make any of the decisions you've said should be made jointly. Your LPA will stop working for those decisions unless you appoint at least one replacement attorney (in section 4). Your original attorneys will still be able to make any of the other decisions alongside your replacement attorneys.

Help?

For help with this section, see the Guide, part A3.

If you choose 'jointly for some decisions...', you may want to take legal advice, particularly if the examples in part A3 of the Guide don't match your needs.

Section 4
Replacement attorneys

This section is optional, but we recommend you consider it

Replacement attorneys are a backup in case one of your original attorneys can't make decisions for you any more.

Reasons replacement attorneys step in – if one of your original attorneys dies, loses capacity, no longer wants to be your attorney or is no longer legally your husband, wife or civil partner.

Restrictions – replacement attorneys must be at least 18 years old and have mental capacity to make decisions.

Help?

For help with this section, see the Guide, part A4.

Title	First names

Last name

Date of birth

Day   Month   Year

Address

Postcode

Title	First names

Last name

Date of birth

Day   Month   Year

Address

Postcode

☐ **More replacements –** I want to appoint more than two replacements. Use Continuation sheet 1.

When and how your replacement attorneys can act

Replacement attorneys usually step in when one of your **original** attorneys stops acting for you. If there's more than one **replacement** attorney, they will all step in at once. If they **fully** replace your original attorney(s) at once, they will usually act jointly. You can change some aspects of this, but most people don't. See the Guide, part A4.

You should consider taking legal advice if you want to change how your replacement attorneys act.

☐ I want to change when or how my attorneys can act (optional). Use Continuation sheet 2.

Only valid with the official stamp here.

! **This is an important part of your LPA.**

You must choose whether your attorneys can give or refuse consent to life-sustaining treatment on your behalf.

Life-sustaining treatment means care, surgery, medicine or other help from doctors that's needed to keep you alive, for example:
• a serious operation, such as a heart bypass or organ transplant
• cancer treatment
• artificial nutrition or hydration (food or water given other than by mouth)

Whether some treatments are life-sustaining depends on the situation. If you had pneumonia, a simple course of antibiotics could be life-sustaining.

Decisions about life-sustaining treatment can be needed in unexpected circumstances, such as a routine operation that didn't go as planned.

You can use section 7 of this LPA to let your attorneys know more about your preferences in particular circumstances (this is optional).

Help?

For help with this section, including how your LPA relates to an 'advance decision', see the Guide, part A5.

Who do you want to make decisions about life-sustaining treatment? (sign only one option)

Option A – I give my attorneys authority to give or refuse consent to life-sustaining treatment on my behalf.	**Option B – I do not give my attorneys authority** to give or refuse consent to life-sustaining treatment on my behalf.
If you choose this option, your attorneys can speak to doctors on your behalf as if they were you.	If you choose this option, your doctors will take into account the views of the attorneys and of people who are interested in your welfare as well as any written statement you may have made, where it is practical and appropriate.

Signature or mark

Date signed or marked

Day   Month   Year

Signature or mark

Date signed or marked

Day   Month   Year

Witness
The witness must not be an attorney or replacement attorney appointed under this LPA, and must be aged 18 or over.

Signature or mark

Full name of witness

Address

Postcode

Only valid with the official stamp here.

LP1H Health and welfare (07.15)

Section 6
People to notify when the LPA is registered

This section is optional

You can let people know that you're going to register your LPA. They can raise any concerns they have about the LPA – for example, if there was any pressure or fraud in making it.

When the LPA is registered, the person applying to register (you or one of your attorneys) must send a notice to each 'person to notify'.

You can't put your attorneys or replacement attorneys here.

People to notify can object to the LPA, but only for certain reasons (listed in the notification form LP3). After that, they are no longer involved in the LPA. Choose people who care about your best interests and who would be willing to speak up if they were concerned.

Help?

For help with this section, see the Guide, part A6.

Title | First names

Last name

Address

Postcode

Title | First names

Last name

Address

Postcode

Title | First names

Last name

Address

Postcode

Title | First names

Last name

Address

Postcode

☐ I want to appoint another person to notify (maximum is 5) – use Continuation sheet 1.

Section 7
Preferences and instructions

This section is optional

You can tell your attorneys how you'd **prefer** them to make decisions, or give them specific **instructions** which they must follow when making decisions.

Most people leave this page blank – you can just talk to your attorneys so they understand how you want them to make decisions for you.

Preferences

Your attorneys don't have to follow your preferences but they should keep them in mind. For examples of preferences, see the Guide, part A7.

Help?

For help with this section, see the Guide, part A7.

> **Preferences** – use words like 'prefer' and 'would like'
>
>
>
>
>
>
> ☐ I need more space – use Continuation sheet 2.

Instructions

Your attorneys will have to follow your instructions exactly. For examples of instructions, see the Guide, part A7.

Be careful – if you give instructions that are not legally correct they would have to be removed before your LPA could be registered.

If you want to give instructions, you may want to take legal advice.

> **Instructions** – use words like 'must' and 'have to'
>
>
>
>
>
>
> ☐ I need more space – use Continuation sheet 2.

Section 8
Your legal rights and responsibilities

> ⚠ **Everyone signing the LPA must read this information**

In sections 9 to 11, you, the certificate provider, all your attorneys and your replacement attorneys must sign this lasting power of attorney to form a legal agreement between you (a deed).

By signing this lasting power of attorney, you (the donor) are appointing people (attorneys) to make decisions for you.

LPAs are governed by the Mental Capacity Act 2005 (MCA), regulations made under it and the MCA Code of Practice. Attorneys must have regard to these documents. The Code of Practice is available from www.gov.uk/opg/mca-code or from The Stationery Office.

Your attorneys must follow the principles of the Mental Capacity Act:

1. Your attorneys must assume that you can make your own decisions unless it is established that you cannot do so.
2. Your attorneys must help you to make as many of your own decisions as you can. They must take all practical steps to help you to make a decision. They can only treat you as unable to make a decision if they have not succeeded in helping you make a decision through those steps.
3. Your attorneys must not treat you as unable to make a decision simply because you make an unwise decision.
4. Your attorneys must act and make decisions in your best interests when you are unable to make a decision.
5. Before your attorneys make a decision or act for you, they must consider whether they can make the decision or act in a way that is less restrictive of your rights and freedom but still achieves the purpose.

Your attorneys must always act in your best interests. This is explained in the Application guide, part A8, and defined in the MCA Code of Practice.

Before this LPA can be used it must be registered by the Office of the Public Guardian (OPG). Your attorneys can only use this LPA if you don't have mental capacity.

Cancelling your LPA: You can cancel this LPA at any time, as long as you have mental capacity to do so. It doesn't matter if the LPA has been registered or not. For more information, see the Guide, part D.

Your will and your LPA: Your attorneys cannot use this LPA to change your will. This LPA will expire when you die. Your attorneys must then send the registered LPA, any certified copies and a copy of your death certificate to the Office of the Public Guardian.

Data protection: For information about how OPG uses your personal data, see the Guide, Part D.

Help?

For help with this section, see the Guide, part A8.

Section 9
Signature: donor

Helpline
0300 456 0300

By signing on this page I confirm all of the following:

- I have read this lasting power of attorney (LPA) including section 8 'Your legal rights and responsibilities', or I have had it read to me

- I appoint and give my attorneys authority to make decisions about my health and welfare, when I cannot act for myself because I lack mental capacity, subject to the terms of this LPA and to the provisions of the Mental Capacity Act 2005

- I confirm I have chosen either Option A or Option B about life sustaining treatment in section 5 of this LPA

- I have either appointed people to notify (in section 6) or I have chosen not to notify anyone when the LPA is registered

- I agree to the information I've provided being used by the Office of the Public Guardian in carrying out its duties

Be careful

Sign this page and section 5 (and any continuation sheets) before anyone signs sections 10 and 11.

Donor	**Witness**
Signed (or marked) by the person giving this lasting power of attorney and delivered as a deed.	The witness must not be an attorney or replacement attorney appointed under this LPA, and must be aged 18 or over.

Donor

Signature or mark

Date signed or marked

Day Month Year

You must also sign Section 5 (page 6) at the same time as you sign this page.

If you have used Continuation sheets 1 or 2 you must sign and date each continuation sheet at the same time as you sign this page.

If you can't sign this LPA you can make a mark instead. If you can't sign or make a mark you can instruct someone else to sign for you, using Continuation sheet 3.

Witness

Signature or mark

Full name of witness

Address

Postcode

Help? For help with this section, see the Guide, part A9.

Section 10
Signature: certificate provider

 Only sign this section after the donor has signed section 9

The 'certificate provider' signs to confirm they've discussed the lasting power of attorney (LPA) with the donor, that the donor understands what they're doing and that nobody is forcing them to do it. The 'certificate provider' should be either:

- someone who has known the donor personally for at least 2 years, such as a friend, neighbour, colleague or former colleague
- someone with relevant professional skills, such as the donor's GP, a healthcare professional or a solicitor

A certificate provider **can't** be one of the attorneys.

 Help?

For help with this section, see the Guide, part A10.

Certificate provider's statement

I certify that, as far as I'm aware, at the time of signing section 9:

- the donor understood the purpose of this LPA and the scope of the authority conferred under it
- no fraud or undue pressure is being used to induce the donor to create this LPA
- there is nothing else which would prevent this LPA from being created by the completion of this instrument

By signing this section I confirm that:

- I am aged 18 or over
- I have read this LPA, including section 8 'Your legal rights and responsibilities'
- there is no restriction on my acting as a certificate provider
- the donor has chosen me as someone who has known them personally for at least 2 years **OR**
- the donor has chosen me as a person with relevant professional skills and expertise

Restrictions – the certificate provider must not be:

- an attorney or replacement attorney named in this LPA or any other LPA or enduring power of attorney for the donor
- a member of the donor's family or of one of the attorneys' families, including husbands, wives, civil partners, in-laws and step-relatives
- an unmarried partner, boyfriend or girlfriend of either the donor or one of the attorneys (whether or not they live at the same address)
- the donor's or an attorney's business partner
- the donor's or an attorney's employee
- an owner, manager, director or employee of a care home where the donor lives

Certificate provider

Title

First names

Last name

Address

Postcode

Signature or mark

Date signed or marked

Day   Month   Year

Only valid with the official stamp here.

Section 11
Signature: attorney or replacement

 Only sign this section after the certificate provider has signed section 10

All the attorneys and replacement attorneys need to sign.
There are 4 copies of this page – make more copies if you need to.

By signing this section I understand and confirm all of the following:

- I am aged 18 or over
- I have read this lasting power of attorney (LPA) including section 8 'Your legal rights and responsibilities', or I have had it read to me
- I have a duty to act based on the principles of the Mental Capacity Act 2005 and to have regard to the Mental Capacity Act Code of Practice
- I must make decisions and act in the best interests of the donor
- I must take into account any instructions or preferences set out in this LPA
- I can make decisions and act only when this LPA has been registered
- I can make decisions and act only when the donor lacks mental capacity.

 Help?

For help with this section, see the Guide, part A11.

Further statement by a replacement attorney: I understand that I have the authority to act under this LPA only after an original attorney's appointment is terminated. I must notify the Public Guardian if this happens.

Attorney or replacement attorney	Witness
Signed (or marked) by the attorney or replacement attorney and delivered as a deed.	The witness must not be the donor of this LPA, and must be aged 18 or over.
Signature or mark	Signature or mark
Date signed or marked	Full names of witness
Day Month Year	
Title First names	Address
Last name	
	Postcode

Section 11
Signature: attorney or replacement

 Only sign this section after the certificate provider has signed section 10

All the attorneys and replacement attorneys need to sign.
There are 4 copies of this page – make more copies if you need to.

By signing this section I understand and confirm all of the following:

- I am aged 18 or over
- I have read this lasting power of attorney (LPA) including section 8 'Your legal rights and responsibilities', or I have had it read to me
- I have a duty to act based on the principles of the Mental Capacity Act 2005 and to have regard to the Mental Capacity Act Code of Practice
- I must make decisions and act in the best interests of the donor
- I must take into account any instructions or preferences set out in this LPA
- I can make decisions and act only when this LPA has been registered
- I can make decisions and act only when the donor lacks mental capacity.

Help?

For help with this section, see the Guide, part A11.

Further statement by a replacement attorney: I understand that I have the authority to act under this LPA only after an original attorney's appointment is terminated. I must notify the Public Guardian if this happens.

Attorney or replacement attorney	Witness
Signed (or marked) by the attorney or replacement attorney and delivered as a deed.	The witness must not be the donor of this LPA, and must be aged 18 or over.
Signature or mark	Signature or mark
Date signed or marked	Full names of witness
Day Month Year	Address
Title First names	
Last name	Postcode

Section 11
Signature: attorney or replacement

 Only sign this section after the certificate provider has signed section 10

All the attorneys and replacement attorneys need to sign.
There are 4 copies of this page – make more copies if you need to.

By signing this section I understand and confirm all of the following:

- I am aged 18 or over
- I have read this lasting power of attorney (LPA) including section 8 'Your legal rights and responsibilities', or I have had it read to me
- I have a duty to act based on the principles of the Mental Capacity Act 2005 and to have regard to the Mental Capacity Act Code of Practice
- I must make decisions and act in the best interests of the donor
- I must take into account any instructions or preferences set out in this LPA
- I can make decisions and act only when this LPA has been registered
- I can make decisions and act only when the donor lacks mental capacity.

 Help?

For help with this section, see the Guide, part A11.

Further statement by a replacement attorney: I understand that I have the authority to act under this LPA only after an original attorney's appointment is terminated. I must notify the Public Guardian if this happens.

Attorney or replacement attorney	Witness
Signed (or marked) by the attorney or replacement attorney and delivered as a deed.	The witness must not be the donor of this LPA, and must be aged 18 or over.
Signature or mark	Signature or mark
Date signed or marked	Full names of witness
Day Month Year	Address
Title First names	
Last name	Postcode

Helpline
0300 456 0300

 Only sign this section after the certificate provider has signed section 10

All the attorneys and replacement attorneys need to sign.
There are 4 copies of this page – make more copies if you need to.

By signing this section I understand and confirm all of the following:

- I am aged 18 or over
- I have read this lasting power of attorney (LPA) including section 8 'Your legal rights and responsibilities', or I have had it read to me
- I have a duty to act based on the principles of the Mental Capacity Act 2005 and to have regard to the Mental Capacity Act Code of Practice
- I must make decisions and act in the best interests of the donor
- I must take into account any instructions or preferences set out in this LPA
- I can make decisions and act only when this LPA has been registered
- I can make decisions and act only when the donor lacks mental capacity.

Help?

For help with this section, see the Guide, part A11.

Further statement by a replacement attorney: I understand that I have the authority to act under this LPA only after an original attorney's appointment is terminated. I must notify the Public Guardian if this happens.

Attorney or replacement attorney	Witness
Signed (or marked) by the attorney or replacement attorney and delivered as a deed.	The witness must not be the donor of this LPA, and must be aged 18 or over.
Signature or mark	Signature or mark
Date signed or marked	Full names of witness
Day Month Year	Address
Title First names	
Last name	Postcode

Now register your LPA

Before the LPA can be used, it **must** be registered by the Office of the Public Guardian (OPG). Continue filling in this form to register the LPA. See part B of the Guide.

People to notify

If there are any 'people to notify' listed in section 6, you must notify them that you are registering the LPA now. See Part C of the Guide.

Fill in and send each of them a copy of the form to notify people – LP3.

When you sign section 15 of this form, you are confirming that you've sent forms to the 'people to notify'.

Register now

You do not have to register immediately, but it's a good idea in case you've made any mistakes. If you delay until after the donor loses mental capacity, it will be impossible to fix any errors. This could make the whole LPA invalid and it will not be possible to register or use it.

Register your lasting power of attorney

Section 12
The applicant

You can only apply to register if you are the donor or attorney(s) for this LPA. The donor and attorney(s) should not apply together.

Who is applying to register the LPA? (tick one only)

☐ **Donor** – the donor needs to sign section 15

☐ **Attorney(s)** – If the attorneys were appointed jointly (in section 3) then they **all** need to sign in section 15. Otherwise, only one of the attorneys needs to sign

Help?

For help with this section, see the Guide, part B2.

Write the name and date of birth for each attorney that is applying to register the LPA. Don't include any attorneys who are not applying.

Title	First names

Last name

Date of birth

Day   Month   Year

Title	First names

Last name

Date of birth

Day   Month   Year

Title	First names

Last name

Date of birth

Day   Month   Year

Title	First names

Last name

Date of birth

Day   Month   Year

Section 13
Who do you want to receive the LPA?

We need to know who to send the LPA to once it is registered. We might also need to contact someone with questions about the application.

We already have the addresses of the donor and attorneys, so you don't have to repeat any of those here, unless they have changed.

Who would you like to receive the LPA and any correspondence?

☐ **The donor**

☐ **An attorney** (write name below)

☐ **Other** (write name and address below)

Title

First names

Last name

Company (optional)

Address

Postcode

Help?

For help with this section, see the Guide, part B3.

How would the person above prefer to be contacted?

You can choose more than one.

☐ **Post**

☐ **Phone**

☐ **Email**

☐ **Welsh** (We will write to the person in Welsh)

Section 14

Application fee

There's a fee for registering a lasting power of attorney – the amount is shown on the cover sheet of this form or on form LPA120.

The fee changes from time to time. You can check you are paying the correct amount at www.gov.uk/power-of-attorney/how-much-it-costs or call 0300 456 0300. The Office of the Public Guardian can't register your LPA until you have paid the fee.

How would you like to pay?

☐ **Card**   For security, **don't** write your credit or debit card details here. We'll contact you to process the payment.

Your phone number

☐ **Cheque**   Enclose a cheque with your application.

Help?

For help with this section, see the Guide, part B4.

Reduced application fee

If the donor has a low income, you may not have to pay the full amount. See the Guide, part B4 for details.

☐ **I want to apply to pay a reduced fee**

You'll need to fill in form LPA120 and include it with your application. You'll also **need to send proof** that the donor is eligible to pay a reduced fee.

Are you making a repeat application?

If you've already applied to register an LPA and the Office of the Public Guardian said that it was not possible to register it, you can apply again within 3 months and pay a reduced fee.

☐ **I'm making a repeat application**

Case number

For OPG office use only

Payment reference

Payment date

Day		Month		Year		

Amount

Section 15
Signature

 Do not sign this section until after sections 9, 10 and 11 have been signed.

The person applying to register the LPA (see section 12) must sign and date this section. This is either the donor or attorney(s) but not both together.

If the **attorneys** are applying to register the LPA and they were appointed to act **jointly** (in section 3), they must all sign.

By signing this section I confirm the following:

- I apply to register the LPA that accompanies this application
- I have informed 'people to notify' named in section 6 of the LPA (if any) of my intention to register the LPA
- I certify that the information in this form is correct to the best of my knowledge and belief

Help?

For help with this section, see the Guide, part B5.

Signature or mark	Signature or mark

Date signed

Day   Month   Year

Date signed

Day   Month   Year

Signature or mark	Signature or mark

Date signed

Day   Month   Year

Date signed

Day   Month   Year

If more than 4 attorneys need to sign, make copies of this page.

Check your lasting power of attorney

You don't have to use this checklist, but it'll help you make sure you've completed your LPA correctly.

- [ ] The donor filled in sections 1 to 7.

- [ ] The donor signed both section 5 and section 9 in the presence of a witness. The donor also signed any copies of continuation sheets 1 and 2 that were used, on the same date as signing section 9.

- [ ] The certificate provider signed section 10.

- [ ] All the attorneys and replacement attorneys signed section 11, in the presence of witness(es).

- [ ] Sections 9, 10 and 11 were signed in order. Section 9 must have been signed first, then section 10, then section 11. They can be dated the same day or different days.

- [ ] The donor or an attorney completed sections 12 to 15. If the attorneys are applying and were appointed 'jointly' (section 3), they have all signed section 15 of this form.

- [ ] I've paid the application fee or applied for a reduced fee. If I've applied for a reduced fee, I've included the required evidence and completed form LPA120A.

- [ ] If there were any people to notify in section 6, I've notified them using form LP3.

- [ ] I've not left out any of the pages of the LPA, even the ones where I didn't write anything or there were no boxes to fill in.

Helpline
0300 456 0300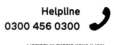

Send to:

Office of the Public Guardian
PO Box 16185
Birmingham B2 2WH

This page is not part of the form

LP1H Health and welfare (03.17)

Form to notify people

You only need to fill in this form if there are 'people to notify' (also called 'people to be told' or 'named people') listed in the lasting power of attorney.

How to complete this form

PLEASE WRITE IN CAPITAL LETTERS USING A BLACK PEN

 Mark your choice with an X

 If you make a mistake, fill in the box and then mark the correct choice with an X

Before you start

You only need to fill in this form if there are 'people to notify' (also called 'people to be told' or 'named people') listed in the lasting power of attorney (LPA). See the Guide, part C.

A 'person to notify' is someone a person who makes an LPA (the 'donor') chooses to inform about the registration of their LPA. They don't have to choose anyone to notify, so if that section of the LPA is blank, you don't need to fill in this form.

When you apply to register the LPA you must tell the people to notify that the LPA will be registered.

You must send a copy of this form to each of the people to notify, before you send the LPA to be registered. You can send them this form or hand it to them in person.

You can save time by filling in pages 2 and 3 and making a photocopy to send to each person.

The donor's relatives are not entitled to be notified unless they have been named in the LPA.

Detach this cover sheet before sending the form to them.

Notice of intention to register a lasting power of attorney

Title

First names

Last name

Address

Postcode

Date

Day   Month   Year

You have received this notice because the person named on page 2 has made a lasting power of attorney.

A lasting power of attorney (LPA) is a legal document that lets someone (known as a 'donor') appoint people (known as 'attorneys') to make decisions on their behalf. It can apply to financial decisions or health and care decisions. An LPA can be used if the donor is unable to make their own decisions.

In other words, the person on page 2 is appointing the people on page 3 to make decisions on their behalf.

When they made the LPA, the donor decided you should be told about it before it's registered. This is so you can raise any concerns you may have. If you do have concerns, you can only object to the registration of the LPA for the reasons listed on page 4 of this form.

If you want to object, you must do so within 3 weeks of the date of this notice.

If you don't want to object you don't have to do anything.

Details of the lasting power of attorney

About the donor – the person who made the LPA

Title

First names

Last name

Address

Postcode

About the lasting power of attorney

Who is applying to register the LPA?

☐ Donor

☐ Attorney(s)

What type of LPA is being registered?

☐ Property and financial affairs

☐ Health and welfare

When did the donor sign the LPA?

Day   Month   Year

About the attorneys

How are the attorneys appointed?

☐ There's only 1 attorney

☐ Jointly and severally

☐ Jointly

☐ Jointly for some decisions, jointly and severally for other decisions

Title | First names

Last name

Address

Postcode

Title | First names

Last name

Address

Postcode

Title | First names

Last name

Address

Postcode

Title | First names

Last name

Address

Postcode

If there are more than 4 attorneys, please make a copy of this page.

You don't need to list replacement attorneys appointed in the LPA (if any).

How to object

If you wish to object, you must do so within 3 weeks of being given this notice.

You can only object to an LPA for one of the reasons below.

Factual objections:

- the donor or an attorney has died
- the donor and an attorney were married or had a civil partnership but have divorced or ended the civil partnership (unless the LPA says the attorney can still act if that happens)
- an attorney doesn't have the mental capacity to be an attorney (they must be able to understand and make decisions for themselves)
- an attorney has chosen to stop acting (known as 'disclaiming their appointment')
- the donor or an attorney is bankrupt, interim bankrupt or subject to a debt relief order (LPA for financial decisions only)
- the attorney is a trust corporation and is wound up or dissolved (LPA for financial decisions only)

To make a factual objection, complete form LPA007 and send it to the Office of the Public Guardian. Get the form from www.gov.uk/power-of-attorney/object-registration or by calling 0300 456 0300.

Prescribed objections:

- the LPA isn't legally valid – for example, you don't believe the donor had mental capacity to make an LPA
- the donor cancelled their LPA when they had mental capacity to do so
- there was fraud or the donor was pressured to make the LPA
- an attorney is acting above their authority or against the donor's best interests (or you know that they intend to do this)

To make a prescribed objection:

- complete form COP7 and send it to the Court of Protection. Get the form from www.gov.uk/object-registration or by calling 0300 456 4000 **AND**
- complete form LPA008 and send it to the Office of the Public Guardian. Get the form from www.gov.uk/object-registration or by calling 0300 456 0300

If you are objecting to a specific attorney, it may not prevent registration if other attorneys or a replacement attorney have been appointed.

You can find out more about lasting powers of attorney at www.gov.uk/power-of-attorney or by calling 0300 456 0300.

Emerald Guides

www.straightforwardco.co.uk

Other titles in the Emerald Series:

Law

Guide to Bankruptcy

Conducting Your Own Court case

Guide to European Union Law

Guide to Health and Safety Law

Guide to Criminal Law

Guide to Landlord and Tenant Law

Guide to the English Legal System

Guide to Housing Law

Guide to Marriage and Divorce

Guide to The Civil Partnerships Act

Guide to The Law of Contract

The Path to Justice

You and Your Legal Rights

The Debt Collecting Merry-Go-Round

Health

Guide to Combating Child Obesity

Asthma Begins at Home

Explaining Aspergers and Demenita

Explaining Parkinson's

Explaining Autism Spectrum Disorder

Children's Health-Combating obesity

Detox Naturally

Finding Asperger Syndrome in the Family-A Book of Answers

Reversing Osteoarthritis

Ultimate Nutrition Guides

Understanding depression

Guide for Cancer Sufferers and Their Families

Music

How to Survive and Succeed in the Music Industry

General

A Practical Guide to Obtaining probate

A Practical Guide to Residential Conveyancing

Writing The Perfect CV

Keeping Books and Accounts-A Small Business Guide

Business Start Up-A Guide for New Business

Writing Your Autobiography

Writing True Crime

Being a professional Writer

For details of the above titles published by Emerald go to:www.straightforwardpublishing.co.uk

Other books by Peter Wade

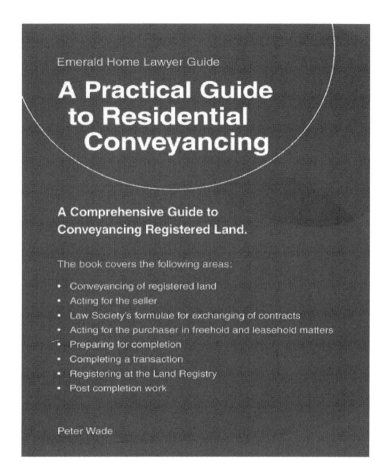

A Comprehensive Guide to Conveyancing –Updated to 2020

ISBN: 978-1-913342-81-4-£9.99

Emerald Home Lawyer Guide

A Practical Guide to Obtaining Probate

**A Comprehensive Guide to
All Aspects of Probate Administering
and Distributing Estates.**

The book covers the following areas:

- Issues with obtaining probate during Covid 19
- The duties of the executor
- Valuing the estate
- Obtaining probate
- Distributing the estate
- Paying all debts and carrying out the terms of the will
- A guide to inheritance tax and tax planning

Peter Wade

A Comprehensive Guide to obtaining Probate-Updated to 2020

978-1-913342-80-7-£9.99